Eng

MW00423928

*An England Travel Guide
Written By An English.*

The Best Travel Tips By a Local.

Table of Contents

About Our Guides - Why They Are Unique 6

Chapter 1: Preface 8

    Non- metropolitan District 10

    London Boroughs 10

    Metropolitan Boroughs 11

    Hadrian's Wall 11

    Warwick Castle 12

    Lake District 12

    Tower of London 13

    Windsor Castle 13

    Big Ben 13

Chapter 2: History of England 15

    The Plantagenets 17

    The Stuarts (1603-1714) 18

    The Dark Ages (450-1066) 19

    The Normans Kings (1066-1154) 20

Chapter 3: Planning Your Trip 24

    Booking the trips to the most coveted tourist spots 26

    Travel Safety Tips 28

Chapter 4: London 29

Chapter 5: South East England 38

Chapter 6: North West England 51

    Manchester 51

    Liverpool 61

Chapter 7: East of England 65

Chapter 8: West Midlands **72**

    Birmingham 73

    Stratford 83

Chapter 9: South West England **86**

Chapter 10: Yorkshire **104**

    York 109

    East Yorkshire Coast 112

    The North Yorkshire Coast 114

Chapter 11: East Midlands **118**

    Nottinghamshire 118

    Northern Nottinghamshire 121

    Leicester 123

    Rutland 124

    Northampton 125

    Lincolnshire 127

Chapter 12: The North East Of England **129**

    Durham 132

    Tees Valley 134

    Newcastle upon Tyne 135

    Northumberland National Park 139

    The Northumberland Coast 140

Chapter 13: Castles & Beaches **142**

    Castles by Region 144

    Must-Visit Beaches 163

Chapter 14: Local Festivities and Traditions **165**

    Cheese Rolling 165

    International Birdman 166

Tar Barrel Racing 167

Maldon Mud Race.. 167

Straw Bear 168

Worm Charming... 168

Morris Dancing... 169

May Day 170

Maundy Thursday 170

Wife Carrying 171

Guy Fawkes Night.. 171

Armistice Day 172

The Trooping of the Colours 172

Bog Snorkeling... 173

Ascot Ladies Day 173

Chapter 15: Local Markets **175**

Gloucestershire.. 175

Hampshire.. 176

Worcestershire 176

Bristol, Bath, and Somerset... 177

North Yorkshire.. 178

London.. 179

West Midlands.. 181

Leicester... 181

Chapter 16: Festivals... **183**

East Midlands... 183

Yorkshire.. 183

Oxfordshire 185

Northeast... 186

Bristol, Bath, and Somerset..187

East Anglia..188

Chapter 17: British Cuisine & Restaurants 190

Some Places to Visit..192

Chapter 18: Accommodations.. 198

London..198

Southeast..200

Devon & Cornwall..201

East Midlands..201

Cumbria..202

Yorkshire..202

Northumberland Coast..203

Northwest..204

Northeast..205

West Midlands..206

Chapter 19: A Few Last Words 208

PS: Can I Ask You For A Special Favor?................................. 209

Preview of "Barcelona - By Locals" 210

Chapter 1: Preface..210

Chapter 2: Benvinguda!..212

About Our Guides - Why They Are Unique

We were travelers really tired of the typical boring travel guides. In most cases, wikipedia is much better, complete and dynamic. When we traveled, we tried to ask friends, or friends of friends who were "locals". That is where we got the best tips by far, the most valuable ones about our travel destinations.

This guide tries to do the same as the "ask a local", but it is (maybe!) better organized and more complete. In all our guides, we hire a "local" writer, and then we edit to be sure that the guide is complete, unique, fun and interesting. Typically we won't add too many maps or photos, since you can have all that on the internet and we like to give you only unique and original content that you won't find easily.

Since we use different writers for each city, you will see (after you fall in love with our guides and download more than one), that they are not standarized. Each city is different, each "local" is different, and each guide is different. And we really like that.

Thanks for being here and we really hope that you like it. Enjoy!

Chapter 1: Preface

England is a beautiful country, with a rich and encapsulating history. From country houses, double decker buses, eccentric aristocrats, cream teas and village pubs, will definitely sweep you off your feet. Modern England is fascinating and an enticing country.

People in England still drive their vehicles on the left-hand side of the road. Whilst the rest of Europe, and in fact most of the world, measure distance in kilometers, the English stubbornly still cling on to miles. England is a country with an insurmountable number of interesting picturesque towns and villages.

You would probably need years to visit all the interesting sights and spectacles this country has to offer. Local churches are grand and imposing, especially in the region of East Anglia. You should also visit England's numerous gardens. This is a unique experience, especially in spring and early summer when the weather is fine.

According to the 2011 census, the total population of England is exactly 53,012,456. Approximately one-third of the population lives in the southeast of England, which is predominantly urban and suburban, with about eight million people in the capital city of London, the population density of which is just over 5,200 per square kilometer.

In England 92% of people are of a white race, while 3% are black, 1.3% residents are Pakistani, 1.2% are mixed and 1.6% are members of other races.

72% of people in England are Christian. Most of the Christians are Anglican, but there are also Roman Catholics, Methodists and Presbyterians.

There are a total of 326 districts in England. Some of these districts are boroughs, royal boroughs and cities. These titles are simply honorific titles and, as such, do not in any way change the status of the districts. Within the 326 districts are 36 metropolitan borough, 201 non-metropolitan districts, 32 London boroughs, 55 unitary authorities, the city of London as well as the Isles of Scilly. The districts are led by a mayor. Mayors are actually elected leaders by the district council.

Non-metropolitan District

The non-metropolitan districts, otherwise known as shire districts, are second tier authorities. They do share authority with the county councils. It is actually the most common district and has its population stand at 25,000 to 200,000. This being a two tier system, the county councils and district councils share responsibilities. The county councils are in charge of some local services for instance roads, education and education. The district councils, on the other hand, are responsible for council housing, waste collection and local planning.

London Boroughs

Established in 1965, these boroughs are subdivisions of the Greater London. Just as is the case with the Non-metropolitan Districts, the London Boroughs are second tier authorities sharing powers and responsibilities with the Greater London Authority.

Metropolitan Boroughs

These are a subdivision of a metropolitan county. Most of the powers and authorities were decentralized to the districts although some services are controlled by joint boards and organizations. The population of the metropolitan boroughs is between 174,000 to 1.1 million.

Some of the most iconic places to visit while in England are;

Hadrian's Wall

Britannia was a colony of the Romans, who built this wall to protect themselves from the tribes found in Scotland. Measuring 73 miles, this outstanding wall stretches from the North of England - that is the Irish Sea - to the North Sea. Its construction took six years, having started in 122 AD. From Wallsend to Bowness-on-Solway, a national path follows the whole length of the Hadrain's Wall.

Warwick Castle

It was originally wooden built by William the Conqueror and later on in the 12th century was rebuilt in stone. The castle is found in the county town of Warwickshire, which is found on a bend of River Avon. Until the 17th century, this castle was used as a stronghold during the period when it was granted by James in 1604 to Sir Fulke Greville. The castle was converted to a country house and, in 1978, the Tussauds Group bought it. The Tussauds Group in 2007 merged with Merlin Entertainments who currently own it.

Lake District

This is the largest national park in England. It is well known for its lakes, mountains and hills which have been carved by glacial erosion. It has a total number of 16 lakes surrounded by brooding, mountains, hills and forested valleys. Its fascinating waterfalls and blooming meadows are a sight to marvel.

Tower of London

This is the home to British Crown jewels but back in the days it served as a prison. It was started in 1066 and before it became a prison it served a royal residence. It is commonly known as the most haunted building in England due to the tales of ghosts purported to inhabit the building.

Windsor Castle

It is located an hour away from west London. It is actually the largest and one of the oldest inhabited castles in the entire world. Queen Elizabeth II enjoys the scenery of this castle most of the weekends for both state and private entertainment.

Big Ben

Big Ben clock tower is one of London's top attractions sites. It is over 150 years old. It takes its name from the 13 ton bell found in the tower and from the man who first ordered the bell. You will be interested to find out that it is the third largest free standing clock in the entire world.

Most populous cities:

London – 7.56 million

Birmingham – 1,006,500

Leeds – 770,000

Glasgow – 620,000

Sheffield – 530,000

Chapter 2: History of England

Since the very start of British history, many wars and battles placed Great Britain under the rule of the Normans, Romans, Venetians, Saxons and the Vikings. In 1066, Norman tribes attacked and conquered England. The Norman Dynasty established by William the Conqueror ruled England for sixty years before the crisis, which is known as the Anarchy (1135-1154). After this, England came under the rule of the House of Plantagenet.   Following the Hundred Year War, England became tangled in its own wars; the War of the Roses confronted the House of York and the House of Lancaster.   The Lancastrian named Henry Tudor ended the War of the Roses, establishing the Tudor dynasty in the year of 1485. Under the Tudors and the later Stuart dynasty, England became the world's strongest colonial power.

The Acts of Union between the Kingdom of England and the Kingdom of Scotland in 1707 formed a Kingdom of Great Britain, which was governed by a unified Parliament of Great Britain according to the

Treaty of Union. The Acts united the Kingdom of England and the Kingdom of Scotland into a Kingdom of Great Britain, as we know it as today.

It is difficult to comprehend how England, such a small island with a small population, was able to rule over a third of the entire world. Its first colony was Ireland in 1169. England was then ruled by King Henry the 2nd, who was asked by an Irish King to send his armies to Ireland to clear inter regional disputes. Since then, the English liked Ireland.

In 1650-1750, the English constantly fought the French who had set base in America and India. At the end of that, the English emerged victorious having conquered these territories and flashing out the French. This they did successfully because they had not just a superior navy and military, but also because of its well organized financial system.

The British Empire came to its close in 1948-2000. This was marked by the exodus of the Palestine and Indians who both subjected themselves to terrible internal religious wars. India and other major English speaking countries continued to remain in a loose federation, which was bound together by the English Queen. This ushered in the death of the British Empire.

England was a country dominated by quasi Protestant Christian Faith. It, however, had a small number of active Catholics and Jews. It then moved on to be a country with various religions from different parts of the world. It is now well known to be a multi- religious, multi- ethnic and multi-cultural state. Back in the days the Church of England preached strict morals but with time started to accept a more relaxed lifestyle.

You cannot mention England and fail to talk of the royal families. There were several dynasties that ruled of England; The Plantagenets, The Stuarts, The Dark Ages, The Normans, The Tudors and many more as we shall find out.

The Plantagenets

The Plantagenets dynasty was subdivided into 3 parts; The Angevins (1154-1216), The Plantagenets (1216-1399) and the Houses of Lancaster and York (1399-1485). The first king of this dynasty was King Henry the 2nd. His father owned various huge pieces of land in Anjou while his wife, Eleanor, ruled the larger territory in the south called the Aquitine. The kings of Plantagenets were the richest in Europe. They not only ruled over England but also France. Unfortunately, most of the French land was lost by King John who was viewed as weak. This was followed by a series of battles aimed at regaining the lost land; the name '100 years War' was given to this war.

It is during this period that the punishments of hanging, burning at the stake and drawing and quartering were introduced. Parliamentary democracy also came into play during this particular era. Oxford University and Cambridge University were developed as centers of free thought.

The Stuarts (1603-1714)

The kings and queens were of Scottish birth. The parliament never trusted the Stuart kings as the kings and their wives had Catholic leanings. This eventually led to war when the country fell under the leadership of Oliver Cromwell. During the reign of the Stuarts, the British Empire expanded hugely making remarkable strides to colonize Ireland, Bermuda, Caribbean, and North America as well as India. England grew richly in terms of wealth as a result of an increase of international trade of goods and the introduction of human trafficking.

The Dark Ages (450-1066)

During this reign, the Romans finally left England after 400 years, returning home to defend their land from the attacks by Germanic tribes. Before their exodus, England had seven self ruled kingdoms; Northumbria, Kent, Mercia, East Anglia, Essex, Sussex and Wessex. For close to 100 years, the shores of England had been experiencing attacks from the Vikings. After the killing of King Ethelred, his brother Alfred went into hiding and after seven weeks, he returned with his warriors having conquered against Guthrum. Guthrum had to return half of England which he had recently conquered. It is after this event that Alfred was crowned king.

The Normans Kings (1066-1154)

Normans were descendants of Vikings. They had forcibly inhabited the North East France. They referred to this land as Normandy. Even though England was easier to defend and wealthier, the Normans liked Normandy most. Castles and churches, which were built by stone, are their visible legacy today. William 1st commandeered the New Forest on the North East of Southampton. This, he made a special hunting ground for the king and his party.

If you want to learn about the history and culture of England, museums are a great place to visit. If you are interested in museums, visit the Museum of London for an unforgettable experience. You will learn a lot about the capital's turbulent past. You will discover how the city changed under Romans and Saxons, and also get a great insight into medieval London. Entry to the Museum is free. Visitors to the Museum can also join free daily highlights tours. Group tours and talks are available at an additional cost for groups of 10 or more people. The Museum is open from 10 am to 6 pm; however, please note that the Museum is closed from December 24th to 26th.

One important symbol of English culture is the oldest lighthouse, which is located in Dover, Kent. The Romans built a magnificent lighthouse, which is now probably the best-preserved lighthouse in the whole of Europe. It was located on the heights of the Dover cliffs after they invaded in AD 43; its purpose was to guide ships safely into the harbour. Known by many as the 'key to England', the great fortress of Dover Castle has played a significant role in the defence of the kingdom for more than nine hundred years, a span which was equalled only by the Tower of London and Windsor Castle. Overlooking the shortest sea passage between England and the rest of the Europe, Dover Castle has a long and fascinating history.

The opening times of the lighthouse are from 10 am to 6 pm.

While visiting London, why not take some to visit the house of Sherlock Holmes? According to the stories which were written by Sir Arthur Conan Doyle, Doctor John Watson & Sherlock Holmes resided at number 221b Baker Street between from 1881 until 1904. This

British government protect this house because of its "unique historical and architectural". The house is open every day of the year (except Christmas Day) from 9.30am – 6 pm.

Norwich Castle is one of the greatest Norman buildings in Europe. This palace was constructed for William the Conqueror during the period when the majority of buildings were very small and usually made of a wooden material. The enormous stone keep was a distinct symbol of the king's might. The Castle mound is the largest in England. The Castle was transformed into a lovely museum at the very end of 19th century. Visitors to the Castle will visit many galleries packed with treasures, such as archaeology, paintings and sculptures from the time of old Egypt to more recent history.

If you love nature at its best, visit Lulworth Cove in Dorset. It is without a shadow of a doubt one of the planet's best examples of a cove. It was formed through sea erosion over millions of years and is a place everybody simply has to see at least once.

Cheddar Gorge in Somerset is England's deepest gorge, at the Mendip Hills' southern edge, its limestone cliff walls rise to almost 200 meters. If you enjoy rock climbing, this is the place for you.

Chapter 3: Planning Your Trip

It is always a good idea to plan ahead. The same should be applied to planning your trip to England. I suggest you to plan your itinerary in advance but always be willing to change your plans if an interesting opportunity arises.

The tap water in England is perfectly ok to drink. It is tasty, potable and cool. Standards of food hygiene are kept very high and extremely strict.

When going to England, don't forget to pack your suitcase for all types of weather, even if you plan to visit in the summer. The weather is very unpredictable here and it rains a lot all through the year. If you are going to England by plane, don't forget to check the websites of specific airline companies for discounted prices. If you book tickets a few months ahead, you could really get great discounts. If you are interested in saving money, plan your trip for months like March, April, September and October. The rates are much lower than they are in the May - August period because of the school holidays. It is always a good idea to fly during the week, from Monday to Thursday. The plane tickets on weekends are considerably more expensive.

Foreign money can be exchanged at the banks, exchange bureau offices, airports and most of the hotels. Keep in mind that banks and airports offer the best exchange rates, while hotels usually tend to have the worst rates, so try to avoid exchanging your money there. ATMs are located practically everywhere and your home debit card and credit cards can easily be used to withdraw money from your bank account. American Express, Diners Club, Visa and MasterCard are all widely accepted.

When it comes to getting around England, rail is a great way to go. England's trains and rail network are very modern and quite efficient. The lines cover all large cities and most of smaller regional towns. It is very simple to buy a train ticket for any departure point to any destination on the National Rail network at any train station. Prices vary greatly depending on of factors such as the distance, time of travel and the operator. I advise you to book your train ticket in advance because the price will be considerably lower in that case. You can do this on a number of websites - www.nationalrail.co.uk is the most popular, there is also www.thetrainline.com. If you prefer buses, you will be just fine. Public buses in England are mostly run by private companies. Buses are an excellent and cheap way to get around cities and towns, it's important to emphasize that buses in England are very reliable and they run regularly. Every city in England has a local bus service.

Booking the trips to the most coveted tourist spots

When you are visiting England, you should remember that there are many beautiful places to visit. One of them is magical Isle of Wight, widely known to lovers of rock-music as a "European Woodstock". This is where such rock legends as Hendrix, Leonard Cohen and The Doors have performed in 1970. Beach lovers will take pleasure in the sandy coast and enticing rocky beaches. The whole island has a nostalgic and almost dreamy feel.

If you plan to visit England, the summer and late spring are the best times to do that. Late fall and winter are usually very cold, quite windy, and sometimes extremely rainy. Summer in England has a mild climate, and you will almost definitely avoid heat waves. If you are planning to travel in winter, you'd better braise yourself to the cold England weather. The coastal areas seem to escape the terrible frosts and always remain milder as compared to other regions. However, if there is wind blowing from east to west then be ready for some chilly weather. A waterproof jacket, hiking boots, as well as some gaiters are a must carry as it is normally wet and muddy. Also be certain to make early bookings, as most bed and breakfasts close up starting from early December until mid March when trips to the countryside take a hike. Some of the interesting activities you can undertake include skiing and snowboarding.

Travel Safety Tips

• In case of emergency, the number to reach an ambulance or the police is 999.

• Remember that cars drive on the left when you're crossing the street.

Chapter 4: London

London is the capital of England and most-populous city in the country and the UK. Standing on the River Thames, London has been a major settlement for two millennia, its well dated history going back to its founding by the Romans, who originally named it Londinium.

Credits: The Library of Congress

London is also a leading global city, with a magnificent reputation for fine arts, strong commerce, fashion, education, finance, tourism, entertainment, healthcare, professional services, media, research and development and transport, which all contribute to its prominence. London is also one of the leading centers of finance of the modern world. London is a cultural capital of the world and is the world's most-visited city as measured by the number of international arrivals; it has the world's largest city airport system which is measured by passenger traffic alone. London's forty three universities form the largest concentration of higher education institutes in Europe. In the summer of 2012, London became the first town in the entire globe which hosted a Summer Olympic Games three times. London has a diverse range of people and cultures, and approximately three hundred and fifty different languages are being spoken in London today.

The city has an impeccable international air transport center with the biggest city air space in the globe. Eight airports use the word London in their name, but most traffic mainly will pass through six of these. London Heathrow Airport, in Hillingdon, West London, is the busiest airport in the whole world with respect to international traffic; it is also the major hub for the famous British company and the pride of England, British Airways.

London has one of the largest transport systems in the entire world ranging from the double- decker buses as well as the river and road networks across the city's 32 boroughs. If you are looking for a sightseeing opportunity then the bus should be the way to go. They are cheap and a fun to learn your way around. You cannot pay bus fare with cash; instead, a visitor Oyster Card, an Oyster card, a travel card or a contactless payment card is used. Children under the age of 11 do not pay any bus fare. This also applies to those who use wheelchairs. If you have a bus pass from another English Council, you may as well use it to travel for free.

Looking to travel to and from central London? Why not try the London Underground rail network otherwise known as the 'Lube'? It is totally amazing. London is served by 12 lubes, Docklands Light Railway and a local train network. They all operate from 5am till midnight from Monday to Saturday. On Sunday the operating hours are reduced. A 24 hour system will soon be put in place. As cash is the most expensive way to pay, most people prefer to use their oyster card or contactless payment cards. If considering taking the lube, it is best that you avoid the rush hours if possible. Make sure to check the front of the train for correct destination. If standing, do not forget to hold onto the rails.

If you enjoy the blue scenery of water bodies, then you should consider using the London River Bus Services. You will beat traffic and get to know more of London. These services are most common with commuters and first visitors to London. What's even more fascinating is that most of the buses will offer you refreshments during the tour. You can pay for the services using your oyster card. Children aged 5 years and below do not have to pay.

And who can miss the iconic London black cabs? Your London experience is not complete until you take a ride in one of these. Keep in mind that if you take a cab from Heathrow or book by telephone, on Christmas or

New Year's Eve then you will have to make additional charges. Before your trip starts, make sure to check with the driver to ascertain whether he takes credit or debit card. Beware of the additional charges attracted by card payment. Do not take unbooked cabs as they are illegal, unlicensed and uninsured. Only taxis can be halted by customers.

If you are enticed by good food and a romantic atmosphere, visit "Andrew Edmunds". Be sure to make reservation first, though. "Andrew Edmunds" is the kind of place that draws crowds, the reasons being traditional and fine English cuisine. In this nice romantic restaurant, guests can enjoy the best traditional English and Irish meals and also savour the various whiskey and plentiful beer brands, not to mention it is practically a Soho institution. Prices are not for everyone, but all things considered, they are quite reasonable.

Want to taste great coffee? In this case, "Bar Italia" is the place to go. This legendary Italian coffee bar on Frith Street is one of Soho's finest places to drink and eat; it is also hugely popular with the locals as a meeting place. It was founded in 1949 when the Italian coffee bar craze started and is still today operated by the founding Polledri family. It is a hub for trendy football fanatics and a magnet for attracting an assortment of wonderful and weird Soho-ites, from cabbies, clubbers, business professionals right through to stars like Jude Law. The loyal regulars of Bar Italia will sample a frothy coffee made with the timeless Gaggia coffee machine that is over fifty years old, or eat a delicious portion of pizza, chocolate cake or panettone at one of the glass bar areas or seats out front on the terrace. The walls are decorated with black-and-white photographs of Italian singers, Italian flags, movie legends, and 50's boxing champions.

What would be a visit to England's capital without tasting something sweet? "Duck & waffle" is a nice quaint place you don't want to miss. Get to the lift and go up all the way to the fortieth floor of the Heron Tower and make your way to the table. Enjoy tasty duck, exquisite eggs, and Belgium delicacies. This place is open non-stop, so you can enjoy numerous delicious meals, including foie gras and streaky ham with excellent chocolate. "Duck & waffle" is also famous for their ice-cream - try few different flavors and make sweet memories that will last a lifetime.

Launch yourself from the O2 arena with an extremely exciting London Bungee Jump. You will get a unique chance to experience some of the best views of London as well as an incredible adrenaline rush. Amidst the famous buildings of the England's capital, you will climb on a giant crane attached merely by the bungee rope which is placed around your ankles. As you look at the amazing London landscape, we hope you will get the courage to take the jump and freefall towards the ground. Bear in a mind that before you reach it you will feel the elasticity reach its limit then propel you back for the unforgettable experience. There is no real reason to be scared because you will be completely guided by a professional instructor who will make sure that you are safe and of course he will prepare you fully for taking the jump. At the top of the 160ft crane they will give you the countdown, then it's up to you. Try and see for yourself how great it is to fall through the air and look at the beauty of the London while doing that. If you are older than 14 and younger than 50, this is an experience you will never forget!

If you get to London, you simply cannot miss going to at least one of nearby castles. You can take a private tour of English castles, with a chauffeur who will drive you from one castle to the other. Windsor castle is a place you simply must visit. It is a royal residence located at Windsor in the county of Berkshire. The castle is famous for its long association with the English and later British royal family especially for its breath-taking architecture. Windsor castle is open every day from 9:45 am to 5:15 pm. The Castle is closed on the 25th and 26th December. There is a lot to see and do at Windsor Castle, so give yourself enough time to make the most of your visit. I suggest at least 2 hours. The Castle is at the top of a steep hill, so don't forget to wear comfortable shoes. The Admission centre is at its busiest between 09:30am and 11:30am, so it might be wise to arrive after that time. Bear in mind that no parts of Windsor Castle can be used as the setting for wedding photography. Mobile phones must be switched off inside the State Apartments and St George's Chapel.

Credits: Gareth Williams

Chapter 5: South East England

South East England is one of the nine accredited regions of England and consists of Hampshire, West Sussex, the Isle of Wight, Berkshire, East Sussex, Buckinghamshire, Kent, Oxfordshire and Surrey. It is the third largest region of England, with an area of 19,096 km² (7,373 sq. mi). It is also the most populous with a total population of almost nine million people. Some of the events of the 2012 Summer Olympics were held in the South East, including the rowing at Eton Dorney and part of the cycling road race in the Surrey Hills.

Credits: Beverley Goodwin

The major transport routes by road are as follows; the M1 motorway in Buckinghamshire, the M40 through Oxfordshire and Buckinghamshire, Berkshire and Buckinghamshire via the M4, the M2 motorway or A2 and M20 running through Kent, the M23 passes all over West Sussex and the M3 motorway which covers Hampshire. They all connect to the M25, which runs near the area known as a Greater London. The main international airport is London Gatwick Airport, with regional airports at Kent International Airport in Ramsgate, an airport located in Shoreham and also Southampton Airport.

The South East of England is a highly prosperous part of England, with the second largest regional economy in the country after London. The most famous university in the region is the University of Oxford, widely known for its ornate colleges and highly successful rowing teams. Oxford has been ranked at the 4th place on the list of best universities in the world by the Times Higher Educational Supplement in the year of 2013. This is one of the most-visited regions of England and the United Kingdom, which is not really surprising since it is very close to London, England's capital, and at the same time is located closest to the Continent.

Brighton is a famous and enticing seaside resort and also a very charming city. It is located very close to the capital city London (76 km/47 mi), which makes it an even more attractive seaside resort. Brighton Beach is the place to be from June to September. All through the summer, the pebble beach is covered with hundreds of thousands of tourists from all over the world. Poi twirlers strike a beautiful image against the sunsets, and flaming lanterns are launched into the air on summer evenings. To the east of Brighton, there is a marked, very popular nudist beach. Brighton has an interesting Museum, revealing the history, culture and art of Brighton and beyond.

Here you will find a magnificent collection as well as enticing exhibitions from artists from all over the world. If you visit Brighton in the spring, make sure not to miss the Brighton Festival, which takes place in May of each year. It is the second biggest arts festival in whole of Great Britain (coming quite closely behind Edinburgh).

If you visit the festival, you will enjoy a lot of quality music of virtually all different kinds, numerous art exhibitions, interesting book debates, and much, much more. For many people, shopping is probably one of the main motives to visit Brighton, but be wise here and don't get yourself stuck in the mainstream shopping area close to Western Road. There is a wide spectrum of stores catering for all tastes, the numerous independent shops and boutiques are something that differentiates Brighton from most of the other English cities. Although Brighton is a pretty safe place, like every other big town it has its own share of problems.

Visitors should know that the city center can get quite problematic at weekends, and West Street is best avoided after midnight. The number of people on weekends combined with alcohol consumption make Friday and Saturday nights on this street potentially volatile. Regardless, it is a perfect place to spend a great Friday or Saturday night at one of the quite places enjoyed by locals and some of the tourists. Brighton attracts enormous numbers of tourists and chances are that you will have a great time. Please be aware that because of an intense and bittered rivalry between the main football teams Brighton & Hove Albion and Crystal Palace, wearing a Crystal Palace football shirt could attract unwanted attention in the city and you might find yourself in a lot of trouble. On the other hand, if you wear a Liverpool, Arsenal or Manchester United shirt, you will not experience any problems. When you visit Brighton, make sure to see the Hillier Gardens. It is a unique array of plants and trees from all over the world, mostly from Europe. You can enjoy a gentle and quiet walk there in beautiful and peaceful surroundings.

Brightons' must-see attraction is the beautiful Royal Pavilion, the marvellous palace of Prince George, later Prince Regent and then King George IV. It is probably one of the finest examples of early 19th-century chinoiserie anywhere in Europe and an apt symbol of Brighton's reputation for decadence.

Brighton's music scene is widely known for its great innovation, variety and brilliant crowds. Live music is a way of life in Brighton and well-known DJs are always in town. Clubbers travel from many different towns and cities here for a night out in the city. On any one night, you can choose between soul music, nineties music, R 'n' B, Jazz, techno, eighties, funk, indie, sixties, house and salsa music. They really do have something to cater for everyone's varied music tastes.

Canterbury is located in the heart of south-east England. It is without a doubt, a very popular tourist destination and one of the most-visited cities in England. Canterbury is an important tourist center. The city was heavily attacked and bombed during the Second World War but still contains many ancient buildings and modern constructions. It is a widely known fact that the city's economy is very reliant upon tourism. Many historical structures surround the area, including a city wall from the Roman times, which was rebuilt in the 14th century; the ruins of the famous St Augustine's Abbey; and a Norman castle, along with probably the oldest school in England. Canterbury Cathedral is considered to be the Mother Church of the Anglican Communion and is also the seat of the Archbishop of Canterbury. It was founded in the year 597 by Augustine.

It has more than one million visitors per year, so we can safely claim that it is one of the most visited places in the country. Services are being held at the Cathedral a few times a day. Canterbury is well connected by the rail. It has two railway stations, one being named Canterbury West and the other one

Canterbury East. Both stations are operated by Southeastern rail.

While visiting England, you just have to have a go at an extreme sport on Greatstone Beach in Kent. Also called land sailing, this is the ideal way to use the force of the wind for some high-speed action whilst keeping completely dry.

Land yachts have been around for hundreds of years, made of wood and appearing in paintings from the 16th century and before. The sport as it is known now has only been around since the 1950's. Nowadays the yachts are mostly made of fibreglass and carbon fibre, making them very modern, quite light, super-fast and capable of reaching speeds in better than 40 mph. The truth is, a lot depends on the weather conditions, but since yachts can travel at three or four times the wind speed even on just a breezy day, you'll be nipping up and down the sand at speed. Your experienced instructor will be glad to help you get to grips with the controls before you're unleashed on the open beach, and with a land yacht to practise in, you'll finish the morning filled with adrenaline and confident in your new land-sailing skills.

Credits: Spiterman

Accommodation in England ranges from motorway lodges to old-fashioned country retreats and from budget guesthouses to chic boutique hotels. Characterful old buildings – former coaching inns in towns, converted mansions and manor houses in rural areas – offer heaps of historic atmosphere. Nearly all tourist offices will reserve rooms for you. In some areas you pay a deposit that's deducted from your first night's bill (usually ten percent). Also useful is the "Book-a-bed-ahead" scheme, which reserves accommodation in your next destination.

The city of Kent is full of fine things to eat and drink.. From orchard, to furrow, to shore, to marsh - the county is packed with foodie pleasures. In Kent, people are never out of cooking ideas, or what to drink with their dinner. Fabulous locally produced food includes oysters, fish, Romney Marsh lamb, and fruit. It makes Kent an superlative place to dine. It offers Michelin-starred restaurants as well as characterful eateries decorated by log fires or beautifull sea views. Kent has everything – from great grub in rural pubs, to fine dining and gourmet Indian cuisine. Highlights include famous chef Richard Phillips' restaurants: Thackeray's in Royal Tunbridge Wells and Hengist in Aylesford.

Bluewater Shopping Centre is the largest in south east England .Visit one of the Concierge Desks where all the information needed for an exciting and successful day is available.

Guildhall Southampton is the South's largest multipurpose entertainment venue, hosting some of the biggest names in music, from Pink Floyd & David Bowie in the 70's to present day bands such as Hard Fi, Manic Street Preachers, The Killers, The Kaiser Chiefs and Amy Winehouse.

Olivia May, a ladies fashion boutique with a difference! They source all their wonderful collections from high quality international designers who create very wearable and unique designs. Crafting an individual look and celebrating creativity in the designers and in the person is what Olivia May offers to its customers.

You'll be spoilt for choice when planning an evening out in Oxford and Oxfordshire. Make sure to check what's on section. Oxford itself has a whole range of things to do. There are big-name shows at the New Theatre, plays at the Oxford Playhouse, smaller productions at the intimate Burton Taylor Studio, comedy at The Glee Club, and international music and dance at the Pegasus Theatre. If you are in the mood for some contemporary fringe theatre and new writing, comedy shows, music gigs and kids' theatre, have a look at The North Wall Arts Centre. The summer months bring outdoor productions in college gardens and venues ranging from the Said Business School's amphitheatre to a former prison yard. Central Oxford is brightly lit and buzzing at night; restaurants are busy, several hosting jazz.

Nightclubs, unnoticed during the day, come alive at night, most catering for a spectrum of musical tastes and age groups on different nights of the week.

Exploring the Cowley Road is an experience in itself - another world - where the two principal music venues for gigs in Oxford are located – the Regal and O2 Academy. If you are looking for a good laugh there is live stand-up comedy every Saturday night at Oxford's new comedy club. Rural Oxfordshire has its own nightlife, often centred round the village pub or hall. Chipping Norton has its own delightful theatre, with live productions, films and events for Children. To visit the Unicorn Theatre at Abingdon, in an ancient part of the Abbey once so dilapidated it was almost completely ruined, is a memorable experience in itself. There are cinemas in almost every Oxfordshire town - some with multi screens showing the latest releases. Or you can just sit outside a cafe or one of Oxfordshire's many picturesque ancient pubs and enjoy the food and ambience.

Chapter 6: North West England

The North West of England is one of nine official regions of England. It consists of the five counties of Cheshire, Cumbria, Greater Manchester, Lancashire and Merseyside. The North West has a population of just over 7,000,000. North West England is the third most populated region in England after the South East and Greater London.

Manchester

The largest city of the area is Manchester (510,700), followed by Liverpool (466,415) and Warrington (202,228). The Liverpool and Manchester Railway was the very first passenger inter-city railway in the world, it was constructed in 1830. Manchester - Liverpool is the world's oldest surviving railway station and is 185 years old. Another interesting fact is that the University of Manchester built the first programmable computer, the Manchester Small-Scale Experimental Machine in the June of 1948. The first commercially available computer, named the Ferranti Mark 1, was also made in Manchester and sold in the beginning of 1951 to the University of Manchester. The world's first transistorized computer was the Manchester Transistor Computer in late 1953. Atlas was also an extremely important computer developed at the University of Manchester, mostly developed by a man named Tom Kilburn. In the year of 1962 it was considered to be the most powerful computer in the world.

Manchester achieved city status in the year of 1853, which made it the first new British city for almost three hundred years. The Manchester Ship Canal, at the time, was the longest river navigation canal in the whole world. It was opened in 1894, creating the Port of Manchester and connecting the city to sea, 36 miles (58 km) to the west.

Manchester has a thriving theater, opera and dance scene; it is also home to the Manchester Opera House, which features very popular touring shows and various West End productions.

Take time to visit The Etihad stadium while in Manchester. It is the home ground of the world famous Manchester City Football Club. Initially when it was constructed, it was meant to play host to the 2002 Commonwealth Games. Several events and music concerts have since been held at the grounds. It has a seating capacity of 55,097 and its construction costed £112bmillion.

There are many buses from the city centre that stop at or near SportCity. During special matches the stadium is serviced by special buses. There is ample parking area with a capacity of over 2000 parking slots. There is a railway station in Manchester City centre, where by funs can take trams to the stadium.

Whitworth Art Gallery is a museum you will want to explore. It was established in 1889 and went by the name 'The Whitworth Institute and Park'. It has a collection of up to 55,000 items. Notable collections include textiles, water colours, wall papers and sculptures. Some of the contributors to these pieces of art are David Hockney, Eduardo Paollozzi, and Barbara Hepworth among others. The art gallery has two storeys as well as a basement. It is open daily from 10.00am to 5.00pm.

On Mulberry Street, between Deansgate and Albert Square, is located The Hidden Gem Church. It so called because it is indeed hidden. The church was originally called St. Mary's Roman Catholic Church in 1794 when it was consecrated. The funeral mass of the former seminal Manchester record label, the late Tony Wilson, was held in this church. The roof top once fell in 1835 but was then restored. The Hidden Gem remains to be the oldest catholic church in Manchester City. The structure could easily be mistaken for a factory or even a Victorian mission house. This is because the external part of the church is made of red brick. On the inside, you will not miss to notice the great Victorian carving while the altar is made of marble.

Portico Library is the second oldest library in Manchester City. It is open to all and there is no membership fee. While there, treat yourself to a cup of coffee or tea, which are sold throughout the day, and a light lunch served as from midday to 2.00 pm. Although it is the oldest, it is still in very good shape and very beautiful on the inside. Through the calendar of the year, several events of art and music take place on the ground. The grounds are also available for hire.

Another place that is not known to many in Manchester city is the Piccadily Records. It remains open from Monday to Saturday from 10 am to 6 pm while on Sunday from 11 pm to 5 pm. It flung its gate open in 1978 and is known to be the world's most independent record outlet. It sells a mixture of pop, rock and alternative music. During the Music Week awards, it was voted to be the best independent record store in England. The services are extremely friendly and helpful.

If you'd like a taste of Manchester's nightlife, make sure you visit "Cloud 23". Located on the twenty-third floor of the Beetham Tower at the Hilton Hotel, it offers floor to ceiling windows and provides the most amazing views over Greater Manchester and beyond. Although it operates a guest list after 6 pm, you can pre-book a table on their website to ensure you don't miss out! Cloud 23 is never pretentious. Try one of their sumptuous cocktails, you won't regret it.

"Gorilla" is another modern and popular place in Manchester. It is located under the railway arches of Whitworth Street West in the city centre, Gorilla is a bar, restaurant, live venue and club space. Breakfast is served until 4pm. All other food is served from 12pm until late. In the evening, the bar serves cocktails and hosts a specialist gin parlor.

If you are looking for a place with a great heritage and tradition, you should also visit "Mr Thomas's Chop House". This is a Victorian bar, restaurant and coffee shop which was built over 100 years ago, making it one of Manchester's oldest bars. This genuine Victorian bar with its unique and uplifting atmosphere, friendly staff, and excellent choice of wine, beer and food make it well worthwhile visit.

Do you love beer? "Bar Fringe" is a right place to be then. A Belgian-style bar with frequently differing cask ales, there is also a fridge packed full of higher strength continental style ales. Fringe has got one of the most eclectic jukeboxes in town as well as a beer garden that their regular clients will brave in practically any weather. The bar staff here is always up for a bit of banter - this is a great local hangout. The Belgian-inspired bar offers a wide range of local and imported brews. One of the Northern Quarters must visit places, but be warned, it can get busy. It does have a large outside seating area, so when the sun shines it's a perfect place to sit outside and watch the world go by. You may as well walk to the Peveril of The Peak. It is an old bar that serves real ales. The building is made of lovely green tiles. It opens at 12 pm to 12 am every day.

"The New Oxford" is a great pub and another cool place to visit whilst in Manchester. It's relatively small, but the place has an impressive array of both continental bottles and hand-pulled cask ales. If you can, visit on Friday or Saturday when you'll be able to choose from dozens of additional beers - which are guest beers only available over the weekend. "The New Oxford" offers over a dozen different traditional English breakfasts and you will be offered a great lunchtime range of foods too. At the weekends, there is usually a concert or live music entertainment, making it an ideal place for either a quick drink or a full night out.

"Sandbar" is an enticing place situated in the middle of the main university area. This large bar is occupied by a fun mix of older students and younger professionals. It is also the main meeting point for Manchester's ever increasing community of cyclists. Go for a beer or maybe stick around to catch one of the regular music sessions. "Sandbar" is a warm low-key place during the daytime, where you can get a tasty lunch and many different kinds of sandwiches for a reasonable price. "Sandbar" by night continues the relaxed atmosphere with an eclectic juke box at a volume that still allows conversation. "Sandbar" has a great and long tradition as a pub, so you can rest assured that you will find a huge spectrum of various varieties of beer.

When visiting Liverpool, the city's Cathedral is one the most impressive sites. The grand Cathedral in the centre of Liverpool is the official CofE (Church of England) Cathedral of the Liverpool Diocese. It was built on St James's Mount in Liverpool and is the seat of the Bishop of Liverpool. With respect to the overall capacity, the Cathedral is ranked the 5th biggest cathedral in the world and competes with the fragmentary Cathedral of Saint John the Divine in NYC for the accolade of the biggest Anglian church. With a breathtaking height of three hundred and thirty-one feet (101 m), it is also one of the globes' highest non-spired church buildings and the third highest building in the city of Liverpool today.

The beautiful cathedral is registered in the National Heritage List for England as a designated listed building, Grade 1. This famous Cathedral is open daily all year round from 8:00 am to 6:00 pm (except Christmas Day when it closes to the public at 3 pm). Regular services are held on every day of the week at 8:30 am for Morning Prayer (Holy Communion on Sundays), at 12:05 pm Monday-Saturday (Communion), and Monday–Friday at 5:30 pm (Evensong or said Evening Prayer according to day and time of year). At the weekend, there is also a 3pm Evensong service on Saturdays and Sundays with a main Cathedral Eucharist at 10:30 am which attracts a large core congregation each week. Admission to the Cathedral is free, but there is a suggested donation.

Credits: Dan Ciminera

Car parking is available on site via a pay-on-exit basis. Parking is free for attendees at all services. Access to the main floor of the Cathedral is restricted during services and during some of the major events.

Liverpool

Liverpool, the city famous for the Beatles and Liverpool Football Club, is a town with a great tradition of exciting and vibrant nightlife.

"The Cavern club" is really a fascinating place to see in person. This is the club where the Beatles first started their career. If you liked John, Paul, George and Ringo, you simply cannot miss this place. It's a bit smaller than you might expect, but this place really gives you an idea of how things really began for the Beatles - probably the world's greatest band of all time. Even if you are not a Beatles fan, this is a club worth seeing. Great music, reasonably priced beer, friendly staff and a great overall atmosphere - what more do you need?

"Jenny's bar" is a great place, with good prices. The atmosphere is brilliant, from the minute you walk down the stairs and open the door, you instantly step back to the 80's! It is dark, moody, has great music and bartenders who are entertainingly mixing drinks with exceptionally great service.

A recent addition to Liverpool's bar scene is "Motel". This is a great place, where the cocktails are excellent, the staff is friendly and the jukebox is always full. The rough-but-polished industrial feel of the place almost makes you forget where you are and, after several of its strong cocktails, you definitely will.

Don't forget to take a tour of John Lennon's childhood home. The tour guides are excellent and they will provide a lot of great information and history to share. Many tours take you by the house, but only the tour with the National Trust will take you inside.

There are several hotels, inns and bed and breakfast points and, as such, accommodation will not be a problem. All these places vary in rates and prices so you are certain to get a place that meets your taste and budget. You can choose to stay one of the luxurious hotels within the city, such as the Hampton Hotel Liverpool City Centre which is only a few walks away from the world famous attractions such as Beatles Museum, Cavern Club and many more. Its location makes it ideal for visitors who prefer to shop and get entertainment in nearby centers. This hotel situated in the city cultural hub has a total of 151 rooms with modern day décor.

Located directly opposite the Convention Centre and The Arena in Liverpool, the Jurys Inn Liverpool promises to offer you nothing but the best world class accommodation. It has a II Barista coffee bar, Innfusion restaurant, Inntro bar and spacious meeting rooms. It operates on a 24 hour basis. You will get safe and secure parking space within the premises of the inn. Whether you are planning to go for business or pleasure, this is going to be an ideal place for you.

If trendy, chic and unique explains you, then you should rush your way to Liverpool ONE. Located in the heartbeat centre of Liverpool, it provides shoppers with international famous designs from all over. Find selected fashion as well as beauty stores on the Metquarter such as Hugo Boss, Armani Exchange and MAC. The famed designer boutiques Cricket and Vivienne Westwood are found in Cavern Quarter. Mega stores such as Marks and Spencer, as well as Forever 21, can be found in the City Central BID. Bold street was accorded one of the best shopping streets in England. Why not stride along the street to find out why?

If you are street market sort of person then you should walk down Lark Lane where you will also find numerous bohemian boutiques.

Chapter 7: East of England

The East of England is one of nine official regions of England. This region includes counties of Cambridgeshire, Bedfordshire, Essex, Hertfordshire, Suffolk and Norfolk. Essex has the highest population in the region. Its population at the 2011 census was 5,847,000. This region of England is well-covered by the Highways Agency. Major roads servicing this region include the M1 motorway from Milton Keynes to Luton, the M11 Cambridge to London, The gigantic M25, which is the London ring road; A1 Peterborough to London; the A5 from Milton Keynes to St Albans; the A11 from Norwich to London; A12 Great Yarmouth to London; A14 Rugby to Felixstowe; the A47 from Nuneaton to Great Yarmouth; and the A120 Stansted to Harwich. There are numerous proposed road developments throughout the region.

The region is serviced by Network Rail West Anglia and Great Eastern, as well as parts of the North London Line and Thameside, the East Coast Main Line and West Coast Main Line. Major rail lines will run from

London to Norwich, London to Cambridge and King's Lynn, and London to Southend with a number of rural branch lines servicing the wider region. A major freight route also runs between the Port of Felixstowe and London.

The East of England is historically a rural region of small charming, market towns and picturesque villages. Proximity to the capital city and good farming has long made the region relatively prosperous, and much of the southern area of the region now serves as a base for commuters to London.

Cities of the region:

Cambridge (Cambridgeshire)

Ely (Cambridgeshire)

Norwich (Norfolk)

Peterborough (Cambridgeshire)

St Albans (Hertfordshire).

The region has five public international airports; London Stansted Airport, which was previously known to some as RAF Stansted Mountfitchet; Cambridge International Airport; London Luton Airport; London Southend Airport, which was previously known as RAF Rochford; and Norwich International Airport, previously RAF Horsham St Faith.

Summer and late spring are the best times to visit East Anglia. Late fall and winter can be cold, windy, and rainy, even though this is England's driest region. The crisp, frosty days here are quite beautiful.

To escape the crowds, avoid the popular Norfolk Broads in late July and August. You can't visit most of the Cambridge colleges during exam period (late May to mid-June), and the competition for hotel rooms heats up during graduation week (late June).

The Aldeburgh Festival of Music and the Arts, one of the biggest events on the British classical music calendar and this takes place in June.

Cambridge is the place to visit when you find yourself in East Anglia. With the spires of its university buildings framed by towering trees, expansive meadows, its medieval streets and passages enhanced by gardens and riverbanks, the city of Cambridge is among the most beautiful in England. The city predates the Roman occupation of Britain, but there is still some mystery over exactly how the university was founded. The most widely accepted story is that it was established in 1209 by a pair of scholars from Oxford, who left their university in protest over the wrongful execution of a colleague for murder. The town reveals itself quite slowly and gradually, filled with ancient courtyards, tiny gardens, imposing classically architectured buildings, alleyways that lead past ancient churches, and wisteria type hanging facades. Perhaps the best views are from the Backs, the green parkland that extends along the River Cam located behind several colleges.

While in East of England, take time to walk in at the Chelmsford shopping centre. You will be certain to get first class shopping facilities while at this bustling city centre. It has been set in a river and parkland setting, which will certainly sweep you off your feet. Another place to check out for the latest trends in the market is the Intu Lakeside Shoppig Centre in Essex. The complex opens at 9.00 am and closes at 11.00pm. The stores at this complex accept both payment by cash and card. Get amazing offers as you walk through the different shops. Fashion designer fragrances and clothes are available at reasonable prices. Also find amazing items at Market Gates Shopping Centre, which opens at 9 am to 5.30 pm Monday to Saturday and 10 am to 4 pm on Sunday and on holidays.

 The shopping complex house over 40 stores such as JD, Card Factory, Iceland, FLAAZ, New Look and many more. Often the stores have offers on their wares but you will only get to find out which ones when you visit the centre. There are a total of 494 car parking spaces. With an ATM facility withing the centre, Market Gates is definately the place to be.

If you love French cuisine then you should step foot at Cafe Rouge. This chic French restaurant offers delicious classic French dishes coupled with a contemporary twist. The shop opens at 9 am till 11 pm.

Are you wondering where to stay while in East England? There are various accomodation facilities that will suit your budget and tastes. Find welcoming guest houses, modern hotels, cosy bed and breakfasts, inns, camping sites and amazing cottages. Spend grea nights and days on boating holiday. Breathe fesh air while enjoying the beautiful water body scenery as you also sun bathe.

Discover the nightlife and entertaining joints as you cruise through the East of England. This part of England dances to a different beat at night. Tap your feet in the different bars and grills in the different towns within the region. This part of England is rich in tradition and you will get to realise this when you walk in to sme of the pubs that are over 100 years old. Ta Bouche, Baroosh Bar and Kitchen are some of the joints in East of England where you are sure to have some good time in the night.

If you are a lover of live music and classic cocktails then you would better rush to "De Luca Cucina and Bar" and "La Raza". The performances there are nothing short of electric.

Cinema lovers are well catered for as Cambridge houses three cenema halls all with stunning selection of cinema from all parts of the world. The three cinema hall are Cineworld, Cambridge Arts Picturehouse and Cambridge Film Festival.

Enjoy a tasty meal in any of the restaurants and enjoy yourself to a cool drink in any of the bars.

360 Champagne & Cocktails is a luxury bar that serves crisp champagne, coffee, classic cocktails, cakes and most definitely afternoon tea. Bella Italia presents you with a wide range of authentic Italian food such as pizza, pasta and grill dishes. It also serves hot and cold drinks. The restaurant is opened daily from 9am to 11pm.

Credits: Nige Brown

Chapter 8: West Midlands

The West Midlands is a county in western central England with a population of 2,800,000 people. This makes it the second most populous county in England. This region contains the second most populous English city, called Birmingham and also some other large cities such as Wolverhampton, Dudley, Solihull, Walsall and West Bromwich.

Numerous notable roads pass through the region, with most converging around the central conurbation. The M5 motorway, which connects the region to South West England, runs through Worcestershire - very close to Worcester - and through the county of West Midlands, near West Bromwich, with its northern terminus at its junction with the M6 a bit south of Walsall. The M6, with its southern terminus passing outside the southeast of the region at its junction with the M1, is connecting this region with North West of England. It passes through Nuneaton and Rugby, which are in Warwickshire, Coventry and then finally Birmingham.

The West Midlands region of the BBC is based at the Mailbox in Birmingham. It is here the programme Midlands Today is produced. This is a regional TV show that is broadcasted by ITV Central from Birmingham, on Gas Street next to the Birmingham and Worcester Canal, with its Central Tonight programme.

Birmingham

Birmingham is a metropolitan borough and also a major city in the West Midlands. It is the largest and most populous British city outside London with 1,092,330 residents (2013 est.). Its population increase of 88,400 residents between the 2001 and 2011 censuses was greater than that of any other British local authority.

The Birmingham climate is similar to a maritime climate, like most of Great Britan, with maximum average temperatures in summer being around twenty-one degrees (70.3 °F); and also in the winter season around six and a half degrees (44.1 °F).

Much of the city centre was destroyed during the Second World War, and the replacement buildings added little to the city. However, since the 1990's, Birmingham has been undergoing a radical change and many of the post war buildings have been replaced. The majority of Birmingham centre is now pedestrian only, and the waterways and canals have been tidied up to make for much more attractive walkways. Residents have given the credit to the City Council for the transformation, as the city retains its industrial heritage while now appearing much more modern and in the twentieth century.

Birmingham Airport is situated just outside of the city, in Solihull, about 8 miles east of central Birmingham, serving the city and the rest of the West Midlands region with frequent domestic and international flights. There are several direct arrivals a day from all major UK and European destinations, and one or two from more far-flung places such as Luxor, Delhi, Islamabad, Dubai, Toronto and New York. A taxi from the airport to central Birmingham will take around twenty to thirty minutes.

If you are looking for a foodie's paradise, then Birmingham is your place. You will get spoilt for choice when it comes to choosing where to eat as there are several cafes and tasty restaurants. Balti Triangle is one such restaurant with amazing curries that has attracted the likes of David Cameron, as well as Adrian Chiles. At the Café Soya, get to sample some of the best Chinese delicacies and a favorite with the locals. The café is located in China town. You will not want to taste any other pudding once you sample Soya dessert pudding, as it can be compared to none. This old town is famous for being the home of Black Sabbath as well as Led Zeppelin.

Most of the accommodation facilities that are fairly priced fill up quite quickly when huge performances are in town.

The Bull Ring Shopping centre is in the heart of the city and there you will find famous stores such as Gucci, Monsoon and a lot more. For footwear apparel why not make a visit to Great Western Arcade where you will find Fly, Dr. Martin and many more? Watch craftsmen making unique jewelry at the Jewelry Quarter.

Credits: Bsou1oeo

A whole multitude of National Express Coaches service the busy airport during the daytime and prices are equal to the bus service. Usefully, the services depart from Birmingham's well-known coach station during the night, which can be very handy for early morning flights. This is also known as Digbeth Coach Station.

Birmingham is a major hub of Britain's rail network. The main station is located in New Street, with Moor Street and Snow Hill running significantly fewer services; however, they do include a service which arrived from a central London station, which is called Marylebone. New Street also has slightly more expensive, services to London Euston which are quite fast.

All of the city buses, unless they are clearly indicated otherwise, will finish at the newly refurbished and much more modern Birmingham Coach Station. The City Centre is roughly a 6-minute walk from the station. Birmingham is well sign-posted and surrounded by numerous motorways; the M42, the M5, and the M6.

The nightlife in Birmingham is mostly situated on and around Broad Street; although, recently Broad Street has decreased in popularity due to the fact that numerous clubs have been shut down. The Arcadian is now more prominent in terms of nightlife.

Outside the Broad Street area are many stylish and underground venues. In the Custard factory, there is a placed called The Medicine Bar. There are also places such as the Rainbow Pub, Air and the HMV Institute. These are large clubs and bars located in Digbeth.

Birmingham is home to many national, religious and spiritual festivals including a St. George's Day party.

The Birmingham Tattoo is a very popular military show held every year at the National Indoor Arena. The Birmingham International Carnival, which is very similar to a Caribbean style carnival, has occurred for the past two decades. Pride - Birmingham happens in the gay village and attracts over one hundred thousand visitors every year.

If you are a lover of nature then you will totally love Birmingham Botanical Gardens. The 15 acres gardens are located in Edgbaston, just a mile and a half away from Birmingham. You can visit the gardens any day except on Christmas and Boxing Day. Over 7,000 different plants can be found in these gardens. One of the oldest species you will find is the Omiya tree, which is over 250 years. This is also home to various unusual and notable plants. You will as well be pleased to find an interesting collection of different exotic birds from various parts of the world. If you want to have a great sneak peak of the birds then you will find them in the white-domed lawn aviary building. The lawn provides a focal point on main lawn. There is a section in the gardens called the discovery area where children can learn and find out more on about plants in the gardens through playing. Throughout the year there are various family activity sessions, shows, outdoor theatre and plant fairs. Every Sunday afternoon between April and October a band performs at the bandstand. You will not have completed your visit without walking into the gift shop found at the gardens. You will get various gifts and souvenirs for that special person. The gift shop is open daily to all and sundry. Not to worry if you are wondering where to eat as there is a tea room selling drinks, lunches and snacks.

West Midlands is home to various famous football clubs participating in different leagues. The various stadia include Villa Park, The Hawthorns, St. Andrews, Mollineux, Bescot Stadium and Ricoh Arena.

Fanatics of football definitely have to visit the Ricoh Arena. This stadium complex found in the Rowleys Green district of Coventry was named after its Japanese sponsor. Although the stadium now accepts cash, it was the first stadium to introduce cashless payment by use of a prepay smartcard system.

Multiplay's Insomnia Festival takes place at the gardens yearly. Some of the facilities present within the stadium include the Stadium Bowl, which has a 32,500 seats capacity. Customers can get access to the different bars and food outlets around the stadium. The 2012 Olympic Football and Heineken Cup semis were actually held on these grounds.

The Jaguar Exhibition Hall is column free hall that hosted the arena's first ever music performance by Bryan Adams. It has a standing capacity of up to 12,000. It hosts the Champion of Champions competition taking place annually. Within the grounds are 121 hotel bedrooms with 50 of them providing an ample view of the pitch. All the hotel rooms are en-suite and customers can get access to Satellite TV as well as Wi-Fi. There is a casino built underground with a standalone show bar. You can access the stadium by taking a bus or train.

If you want to treat yourself with an outstanding meal, Birmingham is the only English city outside London to have four Michelin-starred restaurants; these are Simpson's in Edgbaston, Turners in Harborne and Purnell's and Adam's in the city centre.

Do you like rum? Then visit the "Island bar". Locals highly recommend cocktails at this exciting nightclub, where you can sit in perspex chairs in front of giant blow-ups of Hawaiian beaches and groove to rock and roll. Rum (more than 70 kinds) is a specialty.

Credits: neal whitehouse piper

If you love the theater, don't forget to visit Stratford-upon-Avon. This civil parish and small market town in south Warwickshire is a popular tourist destination and a birthplace of the English playwright and poet William Shakespeare. Stratford-upon-Avon receives an estimated 4.9 million visitors a year. The famous Royal Shakespeare Company resides in Stratford's Royal Shakespeare Theatre. This charming little town lies on the River Avon, which is only twenty-two miles southeast of Birmingham and just eight miles south west of Warwick. This is the biggest and most highly populated town out of the entire non-metropolitan region, Stratford-on-Avon, which uses the wording "on" instead of "upon" to separate it from the town itself. The estimated total population is just a little bit over 25,000.

The town has a considerable number of stores and supermarkets which include a Marks & Spencer store on Bridge St and a Tesco outlet on Birmingham Road.

Stratford

Stratford is twenty-two miles south of Birmingham, which is the second biggest city in England, is very easy to access from the M40 motorway at junction 15. Stratford-upon-Avon train station has excellent links from Birmingham Moor Street station and Snow Hill station, and also from London, with six to eight direct trains a day from the city centre of London.

One of the most popular events in England is definitely Glastonbury Festival. This is a five-day festival of music which takes place Somerset near to Pilton. In addition to the contemporary and popular music, the festival also hosts comedy, various forms of theater, dance shows, cabaret, and many other performing arts. Leading rock and pop artists have headlined here alongside thousands of other artists, which appear on smaller stages and performance areas. Albums and films recorded at Glastonbury have been released and the hugely popular festival receives lengthy newspaper and television coverage. Glastonbury is currently the biggest greenfield festival in the entire globe and it is attended by almost 200,000 people.

Most people who go to Glastonbury Festival will choose to sleep in a tent. There is a wide range of different camping sites in Glastonbury, each with its own unique ambiance and atmosphere.

Hitchin Hill Ground is known to be a much more tranquil and peaceful camping area, while Pennard Hill Ground is known to provide much livelier and wilder entertainment.

Cockmill Meadow is generally a family-oriented spot and is more than suitable for young families or people with children. If you purchase a ticket for the Festival, the accommodation comes free. All that is required is that you take your own tent with you. Don't forget to take an umbrella too because the weather here is very unpredictable - you never know when it may rain, even in the summer season.

The first Glastonbury Festival occurred in 1970 and the headliner back then was a band called T-Rex. David Bowie then headlined the next year. In 2014, headliners of the Glastonbury Festival were Metallica, Arcade Fire, Kasabian, Jack White, Robert Plant and the Manic Street Preachers. In 2015, the headliners included such names as Florence and the Machine, The Who, Kanye West, Lionel Richie, Motorhead, Patti Smith and Paul Weller.

Chapter 9: South West England

South West England is one of nine dictated regions within England. It is the biggest region in area, and covers over nine thousand square miles. It comprises of Gloucestershire, Wiltshire, Bristol, Dorset, Cornwall, Devon, the Isles of Scilly and Somerset.

Devon is a spectacular county with stunning scenery as well as beautiful beaches, national parks, villages and towns. Take time to visit the Greater Dartmoor area which is most famous for its national parks.

Plymouth is a city for family holidays with great legendary history. You will find great live music, art galleries, theatre; just the perfect entertainment for family. Do not forget to visit the great city of Exeter which has its history dating but to the Roman era. While here, you will be able to see the 70% remnants of the Roman Wall.

Torquay is another great area to visit as it is rich in maritime history and known for hosting several sporting festivals and activities. Visitors can participate in canoe steering, canoeing the coves, and cooking your own dinner under the supervision of a sous-chef at the Elephant Restaurant.

Enjoy the countryside lifestyle of the South Devon area. You will enjoy walking on the beautiful coastline with plenty of bars and restaurants to refresh yourself. Its landscape is marked by gentle rolling hills.

Wiltshire is another special region with a great touch of the workings of the Romans, the Normans and Saxons. As you take a walk in this region, you will not fail to feel their touch.

Salisbury is a medieval city and is a World Heritage Site with its outstanding cathedral, National Trust's Gardens and Longleat giving it a golden crown finish.

Wiltshire is an area of exceptional natural beauty and is renowned for its iconic white horses that have been carved into the rolling downs. You can enjoy the beautiful sceneries of this English countryside simply by taking a nature walk, cycling as well as horse riding. Other activities include fishing, golfing, boat trips on canals and so much more.

Get to sample Wiltshire's traditional specialties at various tea shops and restaurants around the county.

And how can we forget to mention the beautiful arts scene covering the theatres, art centers and cinemas? The festivals ad events that take place at Wiltshire are drawn from the past times and the present.

Are you looking to relax away from the busy hustle and bustle city environment? You should consider Dorset. This county of contrasts brims with great attractions and events, it offers the best of the country side lifestyle and you will certainly enjoy its coastline. Visit the task museum, where you will certainly lose track of time due to the numerous activities to be done.

Dorset boasts of its wealth in historic castles, amazing houses and beautiful gardens. There numerous restaurants and pubs in Dorset County where you get to sample some of the best cuisines from Dorset. There are various accommodation sites ranging from cottages, campsites, chic hotels, caravans and holiday parks. Come find out why film makers and writers prefer to carry out their activities in the rich and vast county of Dorset.

The rich hills of South West England envelope this beautiful city of Bristol. Its rich maritime history has enable the city acquire a distinctive identity. It has year round festivals that will leave you yearning for so much more. Spoil yourself at the Bristol Shopping Quarter, where you can be certain to get the latest in high street trends. This amazing city has three all year round markets where you get to shop local organic produce and exotic products from other parts of the world.

You have not had a legendary nightlife if you have not been to Bristol. From live underground gigs to karaoke bars to comedy nights, you will discover that Bristol is a buzz of activities in the night just as it is in the day time.

The residents of Cornwall speak their very own language called Cornish, and the whole region is renowned for its distinctive and rich folklore, which includes The Glastonbury Tor and the legend of King Arthur, as well as its many old traditions and customs. Since the start of the 20th century, the South West of England has been very well known for producing Cheddar cheese, which came from a place called Cheddar in Somerset.

Credits: Giuseppe Milo

This region conveniently lies on several main railway lines. The South Western Line runs from Bournemouth and Weymouth to London and Southampton. The Great Western Line goes from London to Exeter Bristol, Penzance and Plymouth located in the west of Cornwall. The Wessex Main Line covers Salisbury, Bristol and also Southampton. The West England Line goes Exeter, London and south Somerset. The Heart of Wessex will operate from the north of the region in Bristol to the south Dorset coast via Weymouth, Westbury, Yeovil and Castle Cary.

When you visit the beautiful and enticing Cornwall, be sure not to miss Pinetum Park and Pine Lodge Gardens. This is a very colourful place, where the trees have been meticulously graded in size to form a semi-circle type amphitheatre. These gardens encompass numerous features, plentiful shrubberies, water features, a formal garden, a delectable cottage garden, the pinetum, arboretum, Japanese garden and a gaping lake. This garden is really a special place to see, with over 6,000 species of rare and unique plants in the grounds of this horticultural paradise. It is open every day of the year from 10:00 am-5:00 pm except for the 24th-26th December.

Visiting Tintagel Castle is a great idea for a trip. Tintagel Castle is set high on the rugged North Cornwall coast and it offers breathtaking views and fascinating ruins. Take a walk to the stunning beach cafe and enjoy the fine scenery. The remains of the 13th-century castle are more than magnificent. Original steps made from stone, stone dried walls and jagged cliff edges encircle the great hall, which is where Richard- The Earl of Cornwall - resided for many years. There are many myths and still unanswered questions regarding Tintagel.

If you find yourself in south Cornwall, take a trip to Falmouth and visit Mylor Yacht Harbour. This wonderful harbour has a very spacious and modernised marina, which is well shielded from the strong gusts of wind and offers a sheltered haven for yacht owners and for people wanting to enjoy having some time on or in the water. The whole area is protected as an Area of Outstanding Natural Beauty, from Fraggle Rock to Pendennis Castle on the other side.

Pendennis Castle was built between 1539 and 1545 by Henry VIII. He built it so that it would protect the entrance of River Fal and to defend Carrick Roads from French and Spanish naval attacks. The castle comprises of a simple tower as well as a gatehouse that has been enclosed by a curtain wall. It is currently owned by the English Heritage.

Cornwall is home to many wading birds, seals, otters, and to numerous flocks of sharks and dolphins that come there to feed. It is open all year and the Marina has 400 boat capacity.

Credits: Ben Salter

Another one of the great Cornwall places to see is the Museum of Witchcraft in Boscastle. This museum has been located in Boscastle for more than fifty years and is probably the Cornwall's most popular museum. The museum is open every day from the 28th of March 28th through to the 31st of October 31st. Opening hours are 10.30 am till 6 pm and the last admission is at 5.30pm. On Sunday, it is from 11.30 am until 6 pm.

The Roman baths which, located in Bath, are most certainly a place you also should visit if you can. The town of Bath is a naturally charming location set in the rural and idyllic countryside of the south-west of England.

Bath is well known for its hot natural springs and Georgian architecture from the eighteenth century. There is also a small museum located at the same site which includes The Great Roman Bath, a beautiful temple and numerous ornate statues.

The Baths are open almost every day, and they are only closed on December 25th and 26th for Christmas. The opening hours, however, do change throughout the year, and may include later opening hours on the evenings throughout the months of July and August. For most of the year, the opening hours are from 9 am - 5 pm.

Credits: Andrew Wilkinson

Bath is 100 miles (160km) west of London and has excellent rail and bus connections from London and from the majority of large cities in England. Free audioguides for those interested are available in English, Japanese, German, Spanish, French, Mandarin, Italian and Russian. Hourly public guided tours starting from the Great Bath are included without any extra charge.

Somerset is a wonderful and enticing county in South West England, which borders with Gloucestershire on one end and Devon on the other. Somerset is bounded on two sides by the great Channel of Bristol and the local River Severn. The River's coastline faces Wales.

Taunton is just a small city, which took the role of the center of Somerset. Taunton is the county town of Somerset, with a population of around 65,000 people. The town has over 1,000 years of religious and military history, including a monastery from the early tenth century and Taunton Castle from the Anglo-Saxon period. The Normans constructed a stone castle, which was a possession of the Bishops of Winchester.

Taunton has three retail parks in total. The retail park named Belvedere is located very close to the centre of the town and is well signposted. There you will find such retailers as Bathstore, Laura Ashley and also Johnsons the Cleaners. St John's Retail Park is only a few miles away from Toneway, quite near the motorway and consists of two units.

Somerset is a peaceful and tranquil county, consisting of thousands of acres of valuable land, the Somerset

Levels being the most valuable. There is a strong proof of human life from Paleolithic times, and of numerous settlements from the time of occupation of the Romans. The Somerset county enormously helped the rise of King Alfred the Great and had tens of thousands of volunteers during the English Civil War.

Salisbury is predominantly a cathedral city in Wiltshire and the only proper town in the county. This town has a population of roughly 44,000 inhabitants. Historic Salisbury is filled with old medieval stone shops and houses that developed in the shadow of the great church.

Take my advice and join a free 45-minute tour of the Salisbury Cathedral. You will see the clock made in 1386 which has the oldest working mechanism in Europe. Be sure not to miss seeing one of the four original copies of the Magna Carta too, this is the charter of rights the English barons forced King John to sign in 1215.

In the year of 1450, riots broke out in Salisbury. At the very same time a man named Jack Cade led a rebellion through London. The riots happened for many different reasons, although the decreasing fortunes of trade relating to Salisbury's cloth could have also been influential here. The rage-filled riots peaked with the unforgettable murder of The Bishop William Ayscough. In 1483, a large-scale rebellion against Richard III broke out, led by his own 'kingmaker' who was named Henry Stafford, the second Duke of Buckingham. After the uprising eventually collapsed, Buckingham was executed at Salisbury, near a place called the Bull's Head Inn. In 1664, there was a new act passed to make the River Avon useable from the city of New Sarum to Christchurch. It was passed and the work was fully completed, only for the project to be entirely ruined shortly thereafter by a huge flood.

Only a few minutes' walk from the Cathedral, you will stumble upon a small restaurant named "LXIX". It is a nice little place with a modern, cool and elegant style. The specialty of the place is smoked river eel.

"Harper's" is also a very nice place to get something to eat, with the fillet of salmon as a house specialty. The prices here are quite affordable and it is therefore very popular.

There are several excellent links by bus to Bournemouth, Southampton and Andover, which operate seven days a week but a slightly reduced service operating on Sundays. Wilts & Dorset would be the local bus company. They are a subsidiary of the Go-Ahead group.

Stagecoach in Hampshire operates the number 87 to Andover every two hours from the center of Salisbury and also every other journey on the route number 8 to Andover via Tidworth and Amesbury along with Wilts & Dorset. Bodman's additionally operates the number 24 bus between Warminster and Salisbury, which replaced the X5/X4 service that had previously run between Bath and Salisbury.

Salisbury also has a Park and Ride bus scheme with five sites and stations around the city. The Park and

Ride sites are the number 501, which uses the A345 Castle Road to the north; the number 502 which goes via theA36 on Wilton Road to the west; 503 Britford via the A338, also known as Downton Road to the south; 504 London Road; and A30 London Road to the northeast and the number 505, which goes from Petersfinger via the A36 on Southampton Road, to the south-east.

Salisbury railway station is the crossing point of the West of England Main Line, from Water to London and Exeter St Davids, and also the Wessex Main Line from Southampton to Bristol. The station is managed and run by a company called South West Trains. The First Great Western train calls from Cardiff Central, Temple Meads, Bristol, Bath Spa to Southampton Central and Portsmouth Harbor. It runs on an hourly basis every day except for Sunday.

Stonehenge is classified as a UNESCO World Site of Heritage. This prominent attraction greatly aids the local economy. Stonehenge is a monument dated back to pre-historic times which is situation in Wiltshire, England. It is located approximately two miles west of the town of Amesbury and around eight miles north of Salisbury. Stonehenge is possibly one of the most famous historic locations in the entire globe. Stonehenge is where the remains of a ring of standing stones are fixed within earthworks. It is in center of a very dense complex of Bronze Age and Neolithic monuments in the country of England, including many hundreds of burial mounds as well. Archaeologists generally believe it could have been constructed anywhere from 3000 BC to somewhere around 2000 BC. Radiocarbon dating indicated that the first stones were raised in-between 2400 and 2200 BC, whilst a different theory suggested that bluestones may have been raised at the site dating back as early as 3000 BC.

The site and its wonderful surroundings were added to UNESCO's list of Global Heritage Sites in the year of 1986. It is a legally protected and national Ancient Monument.

Stonehenge is managed and maintained entirely by English Heritage and also owned entirely by the English Crown. The surrounding land is owned by the National Trust. In 2008, archaeological evidence discovered by the Riverside Project of Stonehenge indicated that Stonehenge could have originally been a burial ground from its very earliest beginnings.

Credits: Qalinx

Chapter 10: Yorkshire

Yorkshire, the largest historic county in all of England, offers a wide variety of activities for every kind of traveler - from the young and adventurous to the more reserved that prefer to stick to the road most traveled. There is something to see for everyone within the 20 cities and towns found in the county.

The people of Yorkshire have a bit of a reputation (albeit, a good one), amongst other English people. They are known for being generally well-tempered, hard-working and salt of the earth folk. Friendly, with a strong wit and a bit of a penchant for the old-fashioned, many even stick to the daily tradition of afternoon tea and cake. They are also known for their very particular and easily identifiable dialect. They seem to be generally happy with their lot in life, making their lives in beautiful Yorkshire.

Yorkshire is divided into three main areas, officially called as 'ridings': North Riding, West Riding and East Riding. The Ridings are not exactly counties in the politically accepted term, but they tend to be treated as separate counties out of administrative and geographical reasons.

North Riding, known as 'God's Own County' locally, is notably the largest area in all of Yorkshire, spanning all the way from the western boundary of the Pennines up to the north-eastern coast of Yorkshire. That's more than 3500 square miles of a variety of landscapes.

The A1 road, historically known as the Great North Road, passes through the center of Yorkshire County. It is the main route from London to Edinburgh. The A19 road is another important road which stretches all the way from Doncaster to north of New Castle —upon-time.

There is an M62 motor way which stretches from the east to west of the county. M1 carries traffic all the way from London to Yorkshire. There is a rail link, the East Coast Main Line, which runs parallel with the A1 as it passes through Yorkshire while the Trans Pennine rail link operates from Hull to Liverpool while passing through Leeds.

Yorkshire is also serviced by air transport services, whereby there is the Leeds Bradford International Airport, Robin Hood Airport Doncaster Sheffield and Sheffield City Airport.

Once the home of Celts, who were recorded to have inhabited this historic county since the first century, this region has had quite a turbulent past. It had been fought over by a few Celtic tribes, ancient Romans, Danish Vikings, Normans and even by its fellow English countrymen and nobility who all battled to seize control over this beautiful land.

Hardly unchanged from the very start of its recorded history in terms of geopolitical boundaries, it still stands as the largest county in the United Kingdom, giving it reason to govern by itself while still being subjected to British sovereignty.

Noted for its remarkable landscape consisting of brooding moors and green dales that hover on to a majestic coastline, Yorkshire has undoubtedly some of the United Kingdom's finest and most recognizable panoramas. Much of its greenery still has not been exploited by guests and locals alike who maintain its virginity from those who would want to take advantage of it. Its fantastic countryside has been the inspiration for several classic novels in the English language like Emily Bronte's Wuthering Heights and has also been the visual background for plenty of films like Dracula and Robin Hood: Prince of Thieves.

Thanks to the vibrant history of Yorkshire, this region now screams history and culture wherever one looks. There have been castles scattered everywhere in the region since the early eleventh century that either served as a means of defense against the Scots or as a luxurious place of residence that merely carried the 'castle' name to its title. Ruins of monasteries, abbeys and even cathedrals long gone or simply abandoned prevail throughout the region, and only a few historic buildings like York Minster and Bradford Cathedral are still in use today.

Yorkshire has not only largely contributed its own history to the making of the United Kingdom as it is today through its architecture; it has also largely contributed through its literature, which is made recognizable by the Bronte sisters who originated from here. Other authors known to have made their presence known here through their literary works and success were Bram Stoker, James Herriot, Barbara Taylor Bradford, among many others.

Some Yorkshire artists who have made a name for themselves were sculptor Henry Moore, eco artist Andy Goldsworthy, local painter David Hockney, and the list goes on.

Credits: Tejvan Pettinger

Yorkshire is no stranger to the world of sports, particularly in football, rugby, cricket and horse racing.

Its cuisine as well is famous for the rich taste of ingredients specifically in sweet dishes, and its beer is known to have a bitter flavour.

In terms of music and film, this region is all about folk music and dance but is no stranger to the field of classical music as well as that of television, film and radio music. This region is also not new to the field of television, where it had served as the backdrop for many television shows and films back then and in the now as well.

York

Many visitors to Yorkshire come primarily to see York. York was originally part of the Roman Empire, and through many wars and changing ownership, this place has seen a lot of epic drama unfold. This historic walled city could easily be considered to have been the heart of England for many years, and a lot of visitors go there primarily for the historic sites.

After so many years of being a major center of activity, it's not hard to see why York has so many historically significant locations to visit. At one point, York was England's second most populous city, after London. These days, however, the population for York proper hovers at just around 155,000 people.

Probably the most intriguing and famed of the York historic sites is York Minster. The first foundation for the building was laid as long ago as the year 1080, so it's fair to say this building has seen a lot of important moments in history. It is also the largest Gothic building in the whole of Britain and has an especially impressive array of stained glass among many other delights.

You can't visit an historic walled city without visiting the walls themselves. Though the city currently known as York has been a walled city since Roman times, the current walls in place are from about the 14th century with some pieces and parts dating a bit further back. The walls are four kilometers around, and on your journey, you will pass a museum devoted to Richard III, and the Henry VII experience. You will also pass several gatehouses, which are known as bars and were used as entrances in medieval times. Most of the stonework on the gatehouses dates back to the 14th century, but on one of them, Bootham bar, there is stonework that is as old as the 11th century.

One of the best historic exhibitions, not only in York but also possibly in all of England, is Jorvik. At this location in 1976, the Viking city of Coppergate was excavated. Much of it remains buried but the tour will take you through live demonstrations of what life was like for a Viking in the 10th century. It's a can't-miss for a history buff.

If you're more interested in the archaeological aspect of the excavation of Coppergate, check out Dig. Just a 5-minute walk away from Jorvik and you'll learn all about archaeology and get to play in the dirt yourself!

You can't leave York without walking down The Shambles, the most famous street in the city, due to it being a very good example of what a medieval butcher street looked like. It will probably make any traveler happy to be alive in the 21st century! You'll hate to leave York behind, but there's much more to see down the road...

East Yorkshire Coast

East Yorkshire has much to offer in the way of dramatic and desolate windswept scenery as well as large resorts, if you're in for that sort of thing.

If you stop by Bridlington, you simply must visit the town harbor, which is a century old and near a lovely beach. This place can get touristy, so for the solitary traveler, you may want to do a quick pass through the Georgian historic district, a mile inland, and head on down the road.

Two miles down the road you'll hit Bempton, which is a prime destination for bird watchers. There is the Bempton Cliff RSPB sanctuary where one can see many different types of cliff nesting birds, as well as a puffin colony at the cliffs. Some of the notable breeding seabirds are fulmar, razorbill, atlantic puffin and northern gannet. The best time to view these birds is between January and June as they leave for other destinations in August.

If you're looking more for a touch of class instead of communing with nature, you'll want to visit Filey, an upscale resort with miles of wide sandy beaches.

Quench your thirst and hunger by visiting the ever increasing restaurants and pubs around. East Yorkshire cooks and chefs have access to fresh quality locally sourced products from farmers and fishermen all year round.

While at the coastline ensure to taste the breathe taking handmade ice creams, fish and chips.

Get to understand the locals even better by staying in one of the farm stay properties. The surroundings are beautiful and apart from the common bed and breakfast accommodation services available, you may as well get self catering cottages.

Shop till you drop in the high street giant boutiques and small independent boutiques in Hull and East

Yorkshire. In Beverly are a mix of chic and outstanding shops to please both the young and the old. Find all your high streets favorite at Birdlington's Promenade Shopping Centre. Find a range of shops at Hornsea Freeport with various items on sale.

The North Yorkshire Coast

The North Yorkshire Coastline is a long stretch of gorgeous cliffs above a sea ripe with fish, and stretching all the way to Scotland. Take a trip in this county by rail, road, air or water. There are so many things to see and do in the area, it's surely the kind of place you would need to devote a few days to. There's a gallery, a museum, a sea life center, boat tours, and so much more.

Discover the magical sea life at Scarborough Sea Life Sanctuary. Go on a journey from the coastline to the rock bottoms of the ocean through 12 themed zones. You will discover amazing underwater creatures, both animals and plants. Get to walk side by side with the new colony of Humboldt penguins. While here, you will get to have a face to face encounter with sharks as you also enjoy other outdoor exhibits. The sanctuary also saved over 30 seals. The seals are taken to Seal Hospital within the sanctuary where they are nursed until they return to good health then taken back to the water. There is also a turtle sanctuary where visitors are allowed to feed the sharks and rays. The sanctuary is open as from 10 am till 4 pm. It is the perfect play to get an unforgettable experience with family.

One of the most popular destinations in the area is the adorable Robin Hood's Bay, a lovely village with quaint charm that will simply transport you back in time.

If you are in the mood for spookiness combined with history, you're in luck because the town of Whitby can offer you a lot of both. The spooky part is that Whitby was the home to a famed novelist by the name of Bram Stoker. In case you don't know who that is, he was the author of the extremely popular horror novel "Dracula", and the plot of the novel partially takes place in Whitby, which Stoker knew so well. The locals have capitalized on this and there is an attraction called "The Dracula Trail," which guides the way to several creepy locations including Bram Stoker's house.

If you have not tasted the delicious Whitby fish, chips and seafood, then you have not in any way tasted the life of North Yorkshire Coast.

Apart from the numerous restaurants and pubs around, the idyllic towns and villages are some of the best places to find mouth watering coastal cuisines. The pubs come to life in the night time, so you get to enjoy yourself to the fullest. Each and every August, the town is filled with all things music as there a Whitby Fork Week event.

Now for the Maritime history, Whitby happens to be the place where Captain Cook first set sail. Whitby loves its association with Captain Cook, so I would be remiss if I did not mention the Captain Cook Memorial Museum, which contains memorabilia related to Captain Cook and his many voyages.

That wraps up points of interest in Yorkshire. Again, I must stress that there is so much more that wasn't mentioned but is equally as interesting, so if you plan to visit Yorkshire, make sure to devote enough time to see everything there is to see.

Chapter 11: East Midlands

The East Midlands are made up by Nottinghamshire, Derbyshire, Leicestershire, Lincolnshire, Northamptonshire, and Rutland. The region has a very distinct vibe. Those that live in other regions view the East Midlands as being somewhat lost in time, less contemporary than the rest of England, and slightly wild and magic, probably in part due to the large and lovely woods of Sherwood Forest, and the region's association with Robin Hood and his merry band of thieves. In all of England, it is probably the region where you can get a better sense of what it must have been like to live in medieval times.

Nottinghamshire

Nottingham is one of England biggest cities with a population of 305,000 and is most famous for being the home of Robin Hood. Stories of his antics have been passed down since the 13th century and details have been lost; and even though it's not entirely known if he ever even existed, he is still a popular figure, even in today's pop culture. It is also the birthplace of a more recent literary icon D.H. Lawrence, who lived in the early 20th century and is best known for his book "Lady Chatterley's Lover."

There are many fine attractions in Nottingham. Surprisingly one of the most popular attractions there is a contemporary art gallery called "Nottingham Contemporary". It has been a consistent hit amongst locals and tourists alike. The best part is that entrance is free to the public.

Make sure to get the opportunity to visit Clumber Park in Dukeries near workshop in Nottinghamshire. The park is open to the public and owned by the National Trust. The park, which sits on over 3,800 acres, is home to the longest double avenue of lime trees found in Europe. Within the park is Clumber Lake, which is a serpentine lake sitting on 87 acres within the park. The lake has been rebuilt on two occasions, with the last being in 2004 after it suffered from subsidence from mining coal.

Near the eastern end of the lake you will find the Hardwick village. There are bicycles for hire in the park which visitors can use to get around. Vehicle access has not been prohibited so feel free to use your car.

The park is linked to Sherwood Forest and Sherwood Pines by Route 6, which passes through the park. There is a shop and a restaurant within the park. Visitors can camp as there are camping facilities within the park.

Walk through the walled kitchen garden which sits on four acres of land. There you will find exotic plants being grown all year round. There are pathways dividing the garden which contain vegetables, flowers, herbs and fruits. Get to taste one of the 101 varieties of apples in the garden.

Your visit to Nottinghamshire will be incomplete without you visiting the range of Cleverland Hills. The hills overlook Cleverland and Teeside. Some distinctive landmarks on the hills include the cone shaped peak of raspberry topping. Also find time to visit Helmsley Castle, which is a medieval castle found in Helmsley. It was constructed in wood in 1120 by Walter l'Espec who was childless and, upon his death, the castle was passed on to his dear sister Adelina. It has since passed through many hands and as such some parts of was left to decay. The castle is now in the care of the English Heritage.

For those of you that love literature, you can visit the D.H. Lawrence birthplace museum. Though Lawrence wasn't technically from Nottingham itself, the city decided to turn the home where he spent the first two years of his life into a museum. It is actually located in Eastwood. After visiting the house, there is a lovely walking tour around Eastwood. Despite all the effort of maintaining his childhood home as museum, Lawrence is actually not thought of as a hometown hero due to his many scandals and political leanings.

Northern Nottinghamshire

Another coup for literature lovers is the Newstead Abbey, where Lord Byron lived. For those poetry lovers, you can visit the place where Byron wrote many of his great poems. You can also wander around on his grounds, which have pretty gardens and waterfalls.

Your accommodation is well looked after thanks to the magnificent city apartments, hotels, cottages, and bed and breakfast facilities all of which are available year in year out. The prices vary but you will not fail to get one that meets your budget and tastes.

Nightlife comes to being with the eclectic mix of entertainment ranging from classic cocktail bars to real ale pubs. The sweet music and arts will definitely whisk you to another world.

You can find your way around by use of a car, the bus, train or bicycle. Whichever option works for you, you can rest assured to have to most amazing experience of your lifetime. You will not miss a bus to take you around. Most buses are operated by Nottingham City Transport.

Cloud car Ltd introduced the first ever Nottingham's environment friendly cab company. These hybrid cars have the lowest CO_2 emissions in their class. You will also get cabs operating on 24 hour basis. These are mainly operated by 'Where 2 UK Ltd'.

No trip to Nottingham is complete without a visit to Sherwood Forest, hideout of Robin Hood. Though the forest has changed drastically since the time Robin Hood would have existed, it is still a lovely natural reserve spanning 450 acres.

Leicester

Leicester is not exactly the loveliest of England's counties but it does have a certain charm. It has the distinction of being more modern in appearance than the rest of the East Midlands. It recently made world news in 2012, when the remains of Richard the III were discovered under a car park.

Leicester had a legal dispute with York over ownership of the remains and eventually won. The remains were interred at Leicester Cathedral in 2015. Leicester does have a few points of interest, including a clock tower dating back to 1868, which marks the spot where seven streets meet. Leicester also has a wonderful large open-air market that is a huge draw to those that visit the area.

Speaking of Richard the III, the area also has the King Richard the III visitor center, which came into existence after the discovery of his body. It gives a wonderful presentation on his life and yes, his death. They even give you the chance to look at the grave where his body lay hidden for centuries.

If you're in the mood for a more expansive museum there is also the New Walk Museum & Art Gallery. It covers many centuries of history and has an impressive collection of artifacts dating back to ancient Egypt, along with more recent pieces of art. You can stay in Rural Leicestershire which has lovely travel connections to other parts of the country. You will not fail to get B & B's, camping sites and self catering cottages.

Rutland

Rutland, which lies to the east of Leicester, is England smallest County and thus does not have much to offer for tourists. It does however, have two places of some interest. The first is Oakland, which has a small castle and a reservoir called Rutland Water, with lovely architecture. The second place of interest is a pleasant Village called Lyddington that was the site at the Palace for the Bishop of Lincoln in the 12th century.

There are excellent choices of accommodation in Rutland. Enjoy mouth watering breakfast at the homely cottages, guest houses and bed and breakfasts. If you are a lover of modern touch, then why not try the cosy hotels most of which have spas and other beautiful facilities.

Northampton

Northampton was once a very important town in England until a fire burned most of it to the ground in the 1600's. It was later restored but never quite went back to what had been before and became bogged down with the shoemaking industry, whose wares became famed throughout all of England.

Northampton is one of the most modern looking towns in the East Midlands but it still has its touches of history and there are many historic sites spread out around the town and nearby. One of these sites is Stoke Bruerne, which is about thirteen kilometers out of town, but is worth the drive to see Blisworth Tunnel, England's second longest navigable tunnel, which visitors can cruise to on a narrow boat.

For those travelers interested in seeing more of the great outdoors, North Hamptonshire has a footpath of 177 kilometers, which follows the river from Badby to Wansford. It is an even and easy walk, though obviously long. You will not fail to find great apartments, inns, modern hotel, camping sites and other accommodation services. For instance the "Wheatsheaf" is a bed and breakfast about 12.55 miles away the town center. It is in a central location within Crick village. There is private parking as well as free Wi-Fi for guests. The Saracens Head Hotel is also another fancy place to consider when thinking of accommodation. It is a historic hotel in that it is over 400 years old.

Lincolnshire

Lincoln is another small town without a lot to offer to the long-term visitor but there are a few points of extreme interest that many come from far away just to see.

Most notably is Lincoln Cathedral, on which construction began during the reign of William the Conqueror, and which has been added to and changed many times in the last thousand years. However, much of the original stone and mortar still remain. It is a huge tourist attraction, and offers tours that are free with the price of admission. One is ninety minutes long and gives access to a very part of the cathedral visitors can't access without the tour guide.

Lincoln also has a fantastic museum called The Collection, which has a wide range of displays with artifacts dating back to prehistory. The best part is that entrance is free.

Stamford looks like a town straight out of the 18th-century. All of the old buildings and streets have been very well maintained, and more importantly, though it was most prosperous during medieval times, it was one of few such towns that managed to stay afloat after the Industrial Revolution.

Burghley House is an Elizabethan mansion dating back to the 1500's. It is lavishly decorated and, when you take the tour, do not expect to see very many Tudoresque architecture because much has changed since the 1500's due to various owners - the walls are now covered with paintings of gods and goddesses. There's also a heaven room, which adjoins the hell staircase that is painted to be an entrance to hell it is not exactly in keeping with classical themes.

That's about it for the East Midlands. It's plain to see that while this region may not seem as exciting as some of the other regions of England, but what it lacks in glamour, it makes up for with quaint charm, lovely villages, and many amazing historical sites.

Chapter 12: The North East Of England

The Northeast is made up of Durham, Tees Valley, Newcastle upon Tyne, Northumberland National Park, and the Northumberland Coast.

A region often viewed to be on the verge of total industrialization and urbanization, as well as a sort of ecological haven for the number of rare and endangered flora and fauna residing here; North East England is the eighth largest region of the nine regions of the United Kingdom in terms of area and the smallest in terms of population. This region covers a little over three thousand square miles and is home to over two and a half million residents.

Despite its seemingly diminutive rankings, this place is no stranger to the rich and colourful history that is shared by its neighbouring regions, having had a quite early but strong historical past as well as having been a leader in the chemical industry in the country due to the abundance of minerals like salt and coal. Together with its recent and seemingly messy political history, its involvement in the sports scene and its top-notch education system, these all account for a region varied extremely in so many aspects to have become what it is now today.

The North East has been divided into the four authoritative counties of Northumberland, Tyne and Wear, Durham and part of North Yorkshire. Tyne and Wear govern the metropolitan districts of Newcastle upon Tyne, which is the largest and most populous city in the region.

The county of Durham in turn exercises its authority over County Durham, Darlington, Hartlepool and Stockton-on-Tees north of River Tees while the part of North Yorkshire, under the North East, has power over Middlesborough, Redcar and Cleveland and Stockton-on-Tees south of River Tees. Despite the number of districts in this region, only three of these are considered cities — Newcastle upon Tyne, Sunderland and Durham.

This tiny hilly region already had a quite strong hold on religion as was seen in the cultural and heritage sites of Durham Cathedral and Durham Castle in the county of Durham and Hadrian's Wall in Northumberland, as well as in various ancient Roman archaeological sites and artefacts scattered all over the region.

Its strong religious past could also be seen in several early religious texts like the Lindisfarne Gospels, and it also used to be the home of St. Bede who was known to be the greatest Anglo-Saxon scholar of all time.

Despite this area's seemingly strong and peaceful hold on religion, the Viking arrival in the late eighth century turned the people's lives there around and for the worse, having ransacked villages and bringing much of the region down to ruin until William the Conqueror won in the Battle of Hastings three centuries later. Since then, both the Vikings and the locals learned to live with each other, even influencing the locals as is still evident in the locals' language, names of places and even in their genetics.

Durham

The city of Durham has a large Norman Cathedral dating back to the year 1093 and it is the city's most striking landmark. It also has a very large university that was founded in 1832.

It's a lovely city and is somewhat large compared to the other towns discussed so far. Its population is made up of working class people and students at the university.

Most visitors come to town to see the Cathedral, which is strikingly lovely. It was made in the Norman–Romanesque style and has awe-inspiring vaulted ceilings.

Just down the road from the cathedral is the city's marketplace, which has the Guildhall on one side of it and St. Nicholas Church on the other side of it. It is a beautiful area is an absolutely enjoyable spot to visit and is a gathering place for the inhabitants of the town.

History lovers will love the experience they will get at the award winning Beamish Museum. This is a famous open air museum and is opened from 10 am to 4 pm with late admissions being at 3 pm. It tells the story of how life was in North East of England in 1820's, 1900's and 1940's. You will also love 'Locomotion', a museum offering its visitors with the opportunity numerous unique and historical railway vehicles. The museum is opened daily from 10.00 to 16.00. Not to worry about parking as the museum has ample parking for cars and coaches. Yearly, the museum hosts over 40 events such as classic vehicle rallies, antique fairs as well as its annual steam gala.

Before leaving Durham, be sure to stop at Cook Hall, a house that has more or less been around since the 12th century, with some additions here and there. The architecture is astounding in that it is a mix of Medieval, Jacobean, and Georgian, which is an incredibly unique combination. Some lucky soul actually lives there, but there are visiting hours and you can explore both inside and out, where there are several different gardens.

Tees Valley

Tees Valley is home to both metropolitan as well as rural landscapes. There are five boroughs namely; Darlington, Hartlepool, Middlebrough, Redcar & Cleverland and Stockton–On-Tees. Each of these boroughs is rich with attractions and heritage. The total number of towns, villages and cities in Tees Valley are over 170. A glimpse at the fashion scenes, music and ever growing art and you will understand why visitors fall totally in love with Tees Valley. Discover amazing gifts for family and friends at Teesside Shopping Park. Shop from the vast selection of shops available and stop to eat and drink in the restaurants therein.

The park is open to all from 9.00 am to 8.00 pm Monday to Saturday, while on Sunday it is open from 11.00am to 5.00pm. If using public transport, you can get there by bus or train.

Tees Valley is known primarily for its association with the public steam railway, due to it having been invented in Darlington in 1825 by George Stephenson. After the invention, the town focused on rail engineering until the closure of the rail works in 1966. Based upon its history, it's not surprising that it has a railway museum called "Head of Steam". The museum itself is a restored 1842 passenger station. There, you can see Locomotion No. 1, which was the first steam train to carry passengers. There are also some other locomotives you can view along with memorabilia from bygone days of the rail works.

Newcastle upon Tyne

This is more of an upscale destination for the extroverted traveller who is looking for nightclubs, theatres, and shopping. It was once a hugely important town during the Industrial Revolution. After going through a period of poverty, it has bounced back with a vengeance and tourists flock there for the wide array of activities to do.

It is also quite a lovely little town due in part to the fact that it sits alongside the Tyne River, which has seven bridges going across linking the towns Newcastle and Gateshead. Locals generally refer to the area as Newcastle-Gateshead, since the two towns are so close and tend to bleed into each other.

Shopaholics and also not forgetting fashionistas should get to their heels and head towards Newcastle upon Tyne. One of UK's hugest shopping malls, Intu Eldon Square, offers shoppers a chance to get top notch international brands and high street bests. Original Fenwick is a store located within the city centre where you get to shop for the most sought after brands in the world such as Barbour. The five stories store houses one of the largest cosmetic stores in England. The restaurants offer mouth watering delicacies as they source their products locally.

Since its reinvention, this town has developed quite an arts scene and there are several galleries. Most notably is Baltic, on the Gateshead Riverbank. It is awe-inspiring in size, due to the fact that the building it's in was once the town flour mill. It has new exhibitions coming and going all the time. There also classes, studios, various performances, and even a restaurant on the roof.

Ouseburn Valley is another part of town that is full of art and artists, along with musicians. On Lime Street, there are a couple of studios - The Cluny music bar and Seven Stories, which is a gallery that displays the art of children's books and is interactive, allowing children to create their own art to display.

Nearby is another amazing art gallery called Biscuit Factory, which is actually the largest commercial art gallery in all of Britain. Entrance is free and you could probably find anything there.

The city centre of Newcastle-Gateshead is called Grainger Town. It is architecturally beautiful and full of extremely interesting attractions such as:

"The Centre for Life", which is a science research centre and planetarium that lets visitors in and offers a wide variety of displays that are enjoyable for the whole family.

Nearby is the Literary and Philosophical society, which is a public library that also put on concerts and exhibitions.

Yet another art gallery is nearby, Laing Art Gallery, which focuses primarily on British Art from the last four centuries. Entrance is free.

Great North Museum: Hancock is one name for four museums. It has everything from natural history to an Aquarium. Everything is free to the public except the planetarium.

Newcastle is a bit of a party town, and every Saturday there is a party somewhere. To find out the location of the party when you visit, go to shindiguk.com

One of the hugest attractions in the area is Hadrian's Wall, which can be reached by Metro from Newcastle in approximately 30 minutes. It dates back to 122 AD and was built by a Roman Emperor named Hadrian. There is a several kilometer-long stretch of the wall that is still well preserved and many visitors come to walk the length of the wall.

Thirteen kilometres further down the wall is Housesteads Roman Fort, which will lead you on a five kilometre tour full of amazing views.

For all things Roman, visit the Roman Army Museum. It has everything the Roman Empire enthusiast would want to see.

Northumberland National Park

The park is 644 square kilometres and goes all the way up to the Scottish border. One of the most exciting attractions in the park is the Kielder Water and Forest Nature Reservoir. Kielder Water is the largest reservoir in England and there is a lot to do in the area, including land sports like hiking and horseback riding, and water sports like water skiing and kayaking. It is also a good place to visit if you want to catch a glimpse of some wildlife.

On one side of the reservoir is a waterside park that has a restaurant and a visitor's centre as well as the Bird of Prey Centre, where you can see a variety of local birds.

The Northumberland Coast

The coast is one of the most popular destinations in the Northeast. It has beautiful landscapes as well as many historical sites and even some amazing beaches. The refreshing sea breeze will blow through your hair as you enjoy the feeling of the sand beneath your feet. This county has the most number of castles as compared to any other within the England. Some of the castles that can be found along the coastline include Lindisfarne, Bamburgh, Warkworth and Dunstanburgh.

If you are looking to have a lasting impression, then you have to set foot on the Hadrian's Wall. It is one of England's greatest landmarks and a UNESCO world heritage site. The wall joins the Great Barrier Reef and Yellowstone National Park. It was built by the Romans and remains to be the finest remaining monument of by the Romans, as most of its parts in Northumberland remain intact to date. Roman forts, temples and mile castles are scattered in the surrounding countryside and the Hadrian's Wall. Archeological sites and museums explain the rise and fall of the Romans.

Along the coast is Alnmouth, which is especially attractive for golfers. It has a course that has been around since 1869 and overlooks the ocean.

For those of you that love books, Barter Books is a massive second-hand bookshop that is inside a Victorian train station and still has some original parts of the station. It is a wonderful place to come inside and relax, have some tea and browse through books. In keeping with the theme, there's a model train that runs throughout the stacks.

If you fancy a trip on the water, Head to Seahouses, which is a fishing port from which boat trips out to the Farne Islands leave. The Farne Islands are a nature reserve. Depending on the time of year you visit, you may see a variety of birds and possibly a grey seal or two. There is a variety of different tours you can take depending on what kind of animals you're looking for.

Chapter 13: Castles & Beaches

England has had such a long and rich history and thusly, it is well known for its many castles. Unfortunately, some of these castles have been lost to time and nothing remains of them. In other cases, we only have small remnants of what were once massive fortresses. Luckily, due to restoration that occurred in later centuries, we still have some castles that are fully intact and can be toured on the inside. To visit these castles is to go back in time and imagine how people lived in medieval times, when warfare was incredibly prevalent and life was short.

England easily boasts of a long and colorful history that could only come with its many historic sites and landmarks. Not all these landmarks are made by man, though; the variety of the natural landscapes and flora that bejewel this country is enough reason for travelers and tourists of all sorts to come over. The country is well-known for its limestone cliff formations and rolling hills and valleys, much of which have been the inspiration for many classic English novels as well as the backdrop for television and film.

Its beaches are no exception to the beauty that the country has every right to be proud of. Much of its beaches are hidden away from the hustle and bustle of the urban city life, so getting there may take some time but can only be a pleasant surprise and an instant breather for those who do take the time to travel out there. Each and every region of England offers a little coastal surprise for those who want to take a break from the city life, so let us cut to the chase now and explore these hidden beauties, shall we?

Castles by Region

East Midlands
Ashby de la Zouch Castle

The site where the castle lies originated as a Norman house in the 12th century. It was built by Alain de Porhoet but it changed ownership several years down the line. The manor house reached its castle status in 15th century. The castle was a stronghold for the Royalist back in the days during the civil war. It became a famous destination for tourist from the year 1819 when Sir Walter Scott talked about it in his novel 'Ivanhoe'. Though it is now in a state of lovely ruins, there are guided tours, and it is a popular tourist destination in Leicestershire. It is now in the care of English Heritage. The ruins have since been stabilized from further deterioration with the grounds having been laid to grass. There are a total of 98 steps so climbing up the Hastings Tower is quite possible. There is an underground passage from the basements of the kitchen to the Hastings Tower. This is believed to have been created during the civil war era. The castle is open during the weekends from 10.00am to 4.00pm.

Bolingbroke Castle

This castle was built in 1230 by the Earl of Chester. The castle's biggest claim to fame is that it is the birthplace of Henry IV. In a bid to prevent any other use of it, the castle was slighted in 1652. Its walls and towers tore down to and were then dumped into the moat. It is in 1815 that the last major remaining structure fell down. Some of the lower walls and ground floors of the tower can be visible to date. Entry into the castle is absolutely free and is open during reasonable times of the day. Despite the fact that it is in a state of complete ruins, it is still a major tourist attraction, and there are often Shakespeare performances on the grounds.

Credits: Duncan

Kirby Muxloe Castle

William Hastings began building on this castle in the 15th century. Sadly, it was never finished, because he was executed. The castle was impressive at the time it was begun, because they used brick, which was fashionable and not a common building material at that time, due to how expensive it was.

The castle was to be one of a kind as it had gun ports used for artillery emplacements. This type of defensive mechanism was quite new during that particular reign. The remaining parts of the building are the gatehouse and the west tower. The aim of William was to create a residential area of a rectangular plan surrounded by walls, towers and moat. Above the gateway one can visibly see the initials W.H as well as the arms of the Hastlings, a ship and the lower half of a particular figure.

At the ground floor are two rooms which were to serve as the guard room and porters lodge. Today the porters lodge is used as a reception for visitors. It is still somewhat structurally intact, and is a good tourist destination partially due to the Castle Hotel, which is a pub that was built in the 17th century, serves traditional foods, and overlooks the ruins. Some of the activities that can be enjoyed on these grounds include having some nice picnic with friends and family as well as taking a walk on the moat.

Credits: Jeremy Polanski

Lincoln Castle

Construction began on this castle in 1068 by William the Conqueror. It is incredibly well preserved and is currently a museum. It is next to Lincoln Cathedral.

The castle was used as a prison and a court room. It has remained to be one of England's best artifacts as one can still walk around the Norman walls without a problem. Walking through the walls, you will notice a magnificent view of the castle buildings, the city, the cathedral, as well as the surrounding countryside. During the tough struggle that was going on between King Stephen and Empress Matilda, when the first battle of Lincoln took place, the castle became a huge point of attention.

Though it was damaged, it was held and a new tower erected. This tower was known as the Lucy tower.

In the post medieval times, the castle was to establish a prison. In 1878 the system was abolished and the prisoners were transferred to a new prison in outskirts of Lincoln.

An exhibition giving a detailed information about the origin of the Magna Carta and its effects is carried out to date since 1215. Music concerts take place on the grounds of the castle while the public can as well enjoy great times with family and friends. It is open from 10.00 am to 4.00pm

London

Windsor Castle

William the Conqueror built Windsor Castle in the 11th century. It is rare among the castles of England in that it is still occupied and has been continuously since it was first built. The castle currently employs hundreds of people and the reigning Queen stays there often and uses it as a location to hold events and meet with visiting dignitaries. It is one of the major tourist destinations in England.

[For more information, visit royalcollection.org.uk]

Credits: Brian Poliansky

Hampton Court

This royal palace was built in the 16th century and has not been occupied by the royal family for 300 years. It is currently a huge attraction for tourists, many who come to see and walk through the maze on the grounds, which was planted in the 17th century for William III of Orange.

[For more information, visit hrp.org.uk]

Credits:Paul Hudson

Tower of London

This castle was originally founded in 1066 by William the Conqueror, who had it built directly on the riverbank of the Thames. He built the White Tower in 1078, and subsequently the castle became known as the Tower of London. It is one of the most identifiable landmarks in all of England. Few people know that not only has it served as a royal residence, but also as a prison, for several hundred years.

It also has an even darker past and many claim that there are several ghosts lurking in the tower; most notably, the ghost of Anne Boleyn, one of Henry VIII's wives, whom was order to be beheaded by her husband. It is said she wanders the halls of the White Tower, with her head tucked neatly in her arm. Despite the possible spookiness, it is an incredibly popular tourist attraction.

Credits:Joshua Barnett

North East

The highly industrial and fast-paced urbanized lifestyle in the North East region of the United Kingdom is definitely a far cry from the beaches that this tiny region offers. Much of its beaches are quite close to the cities and districts, but it is far enough away from the crowds and the noise of the urban and even suburban life. If you could not easily get away to someplace far, the nearby beaches could definitely suffice for a break from all the stress and the quick pace.

If you are not much for the drama or for the adventure and would rather go for something more secluded but not so far away from the fast-paced metropolitan life, the North Sands Beach in Hartlepool, County Dunham and the Sugar Sands Beach in Northumberland are just the beaches for that.

The North Sands

The North Sands is quite a temperamental place though — you would have to time your visit with the low tide to truly immerse yourself in what can only be one of the best beach walks in the North East. Much of the sands here are quite golden in appearance due to remnants of magnesian limestone in them, as well as in the cliffs where the coastal path lies during high tide.

The Sugar Sands on the other hand can be visited any time of the year and is actually full of trees, rock pools large enough for swimming and amazing rock formations where guests are free to jump from.

Alnwick Castle

Located in Durham, Alnwick Castle is one of the more recently popular tourist attractions due to it having been portrayed as Hogwarts in the "Harry Potter" films. It was originally built in the late 11th century and has been occupied by each Duke of Northumberland. It has been remodelled to the style of each Duke who has lived there. There are castle and garden tours and it is often a very crowded destination.

[For more information, visit alnwickcastle.com]

Bamburgh Castle

Located in Northumberland, Bamburgh Castle is one of the older castles still standing in England. It was built around the 6th century and has changed a lot over time, as it has passed through the hands of many owners and seen many dramatic moments in history, including warfare. The original castle was demolished in the 19th century and replaced with something more akin to a mansion. However it still houses treasures from many centuries past and is worth exploring. Though tourists are welcome, it is also one of the few castles that is still occupied.

[For more information, visit bamburgh.org]

Credits:David

Northwest

Lancaster Castle

Lancaster Castle was built in the 11th century. It is still a very active building, until recently it operated as a prison and is still a court.

[For more information, visit lancastercastle.com]

Credits:Linda Martin

Southeast

Dover Castle

Dover Castle is one of the more awe-inspiring castles in all of England. It was originally built by William the Conqueror in 1068 and has been used during wartime ever since, including as recently as World War II. There is an incredible amount of stuff to see and do on the grounds, so make sure to allot enough time to spend there.

[For more information, visit english-heritage.org.uk]

Leeds Castle

Leeds Castle, while absolutely gorgeous and dating back to the 12th century, offers more modern entertainment than historical information. Some activities available are hot air ballooning and zip lining. Or you can just spend a day walking around the massive grounds.

[For more information, visit leeds-castle.com]

Southwest

St. Mawe's Castle

This castle is situated in a lovely location on the coast in Cornwall. It was built in the 1500's and is in wonderful condition and is in a cloverleaf design.

[For more information, visit English-heritage.org.uk]

Credits:Paul Reynolds

Berkeley Castle

This castle, located in Gloucestershire, was built in the 11th century and is best known as being the location of Edward II's murder in 1327. It is a family home of the Berkeley's and has been well maintained throughout time.

[For more information, visit berkeley-castle.com]

Credits:steve p2008

West Midlands

Warwick Castle

Located in the small town of Warwick, this castle was built by William the Conqueror in 1068. It is a major attraction due in part to the size of the structure as well as the beauty of the grounds, which are extensive and on which sits a conservatory. Medieval themed events often take place on nearby River Island, located by the River Avon.

[For more information, visit warwick-castle.com]

Kenilworth Castle

Located in Warwickshire, has seen many pivotal moments in history, including the siege of Kenilworth, which was a battle that took place in 1266 and lasted six months. The castle was founded in the 12th century and has been built on over the centuries.

Yorkshire

Scarborough Castle

This castle in Yorkshire sits dramatically overlooking the North Sea. The castle was built in the 12th century on the site of an Iron Age settlement and offers wonderful views in all directions.

Credits:Ashley Van-Haeften

Skipton Castle

Built in 1090, this castle has been amazingly well preserved over the centuries.

It is a very popular tourist attraction and is also occupied as a residence. It is a good destination for those that want to see what an authentic medieval Castle looks like because, unlike many medieval castles in England, it has not received many modifications in the style of subsequent eras.

Must-Visit Beaches

The length of the coastline of England is approximately 9000 kilometres, so suffice it to say, there are quite a lot great beaches to choose from.

Devon

Woolacomb Sands

Woolacomb Sands at the resort of Woolacomb has great waves for surfers, as well as the nearby beach of Putsborough Sands. A few miles down the coast are Croyde Bay and Saunton Sands, two more gorgeous surfing paradises.

Cornwall

Porthcurno Bay

Porthcurno Beach is a lovely beach spread out beneath Minack Theatre, which is built into the cliffs and seats 750 people.

Newquay

For those interested in surfing, Newquay is a popular destination. There are multiple beaches in the area, and the best surfing can be found at Watergate Bay and Fistral Bay.

Southeast

Camber Sands

Camber Sands, near Rye, is a major destination for active beachgoers looking to engage in water sports.

Chapter 14: Local Festivities and Traditions

If there's one thing English people love, it's creating new traditions and maintaining old ones. Over the course of its long history, England has developed some strange and fascinating celebrations and customs. Some have become world famous and some are only known by the English themselves. Some are centuries old and others are only a few years old. One thing is certain: no matter where you go in the country, you are bound to find that the locals have at least a couple of interesting annual traditions.

Cheese Rolling

Cheese rolling is exactly what it sounds like. In Gloucester, there is a yearly event called Cooper's Hill cheese rolling and wake. Contestants start at the top of the hill and a large cheese wheel is set free rolling down, contestants all chase after the cheese in the first person to the bottom is the winner and they get to keep the cheese. It is one of those strange traditions that have gone on for so long but no one seems to be certain when it actually began. Over the years, it has become a larger event and attracts more people every year, many who have come to the area specifically for that event.

This event takes place on the Spring Bank holiday.

International Birdman

This strange yearly competition held in Sussex began in the 70's and involves "birdmen" (humans dressed in bird costume). They jump off a pier and attempt to "fly" as far as possible before falling into the water. Contestants wear a variety of different suits created to help them fly as far into the water if possible. Some wear simple wings while others have huge elaborately constructed contraptions that they strap into. The event has occurred yearly for over forty years but has occasionally been cancelled due to safety concerns.

Tar Barrel Racing

Along with bonfires on the 5th of November, there's also the tradition of tar barrel racing in Devon. It is an extremely dangerous event in which men run around town carrying heavy barrels full of burning tar. The origins of this dangerous event are not completely known, only that it somehow ties into the Gunpowder Plot.

Maldon Mud Race

This race originally began in the dead of winter in Essex. As with many uniquely English competitions, it began as a bet, and has evolved greatly in the forty years since it began. It is a charity event and often brings in hundreds or thousands of spectators who watch contestants run through the mud of low tide on the River Blackwater. The number of contestants has increased yearly and often numbers in the hundreds, possibly due to the fact that in recent years it has been held in warmer months.

Straw Bear

The custom of the Straw Bear is an extremely old tradition that began in Cambridgeshire at an unknown time in history. It is a very strange tradition in which a man would clothe himself in straw and knock on the doors of the townspeople. When they answered, he would do a dance for them and they would gift him with food and drink. At one point, the tradition died out and then was resurrected in the 1980's. Unlike some of the other events on this list, the Straw Bear tradition has not expanded beyond the small town in which it began, Whittlesey. However, instead of taking place only one day a year, it is now a full weekend - the second in January - and encompasses many more people that dance along with the bear during a parade through the streets of town. There are also musical performances and dances that take place throughout the weekend.

Worm Charming

Worm charming is the literal act of "charming" worms from the ground for bait. It requires skill and practice, and England turned it into a competition when the World Worm Charming Championship began in the 1980's in Cheshire. Since then, other festivals and championships celebrating worm charming have become traditional in other places. In southwest England there is the International Festival of Worm Charming at Devon. The celebration of worm charming has also spread overseas, with festivals honouring the tradition now taking place in Canada and America in the summer.

Morris Dancing

Morris dancing is a traditional folk dance that dates back to medieval England. It is essentially rhythmic stepping performed by dancers wearing traditional garments, including ribbons and bells. The dancers often weave around sticks and handkerchiefs. There are several different variations on the dance that evolved out of different locations in England. That is not a dance that takes place annually on a specific day, but is performed at various folk festivals.

May Day

The celebration of May Day in England dates back to medieval times and was the manner in which the arrival of spring was celebrated. It often involves Maypole Dancing, in which children tie ribbons to a pole and dance around it. Its origins are pagan.

Maundy Thursday

This day normally falls on the day before Good Friday during Easter holiday. This is a day commemorated not only in England but also by Christians in other parts of the world. It is on this day that they remember the last supper held by Jesus Christ. In England Maundy Thursday is a time to give and help the poor. A certain church in England graces this day by the attendance of the Queen of England, where she gets to hand out coins known as the Maundy money. These coins are made particularly for the poor in the society. On this particular day, the citizens of England get to hand out clothes as well as food stuff to the poor in the society.

Wife Carrying

This tradition of a group of men, each carrying a woman, racing against each other has its disturbing origins in Surrey, and is based upon the Viking invasion in the 8th century in which Vikings rampaged through the area and carried off local women for nefarious reasons. These days it is a much more light-hearted event with very specific rules, including that it is only men carrying their wives instead of strange women. It is a yearly event in Dorking.

Guy Fawkes Night

Also known as the bonfire night, the English celebrate this night by remembering Guy Fawkes. If you think he was some sort of a hero, think again. He is one of the most popular traitors in English history. Using barrels of gun powder, he tried to blow up not just the parliament, but also King James. This was in the year 1605. Unfortunately for him, his plan did not materialise as one of his helpers tipped off the king.

People light bonfires and fireworks during this night. Children participate in the tradition by making ugly dummies from old pieces of clothes and newspapers which they then throw into the bonfires as they pass through the streets.

Armistice Day

Armistice Day is when the people of England get to remember all their fallen heroes who took part in the world wars. It occurs on the Sunday which is closest to the 11th of November. At 11.00am on this particular day, people down their tools to take two minutes of silence in honour of the dead soldiers. In other traditions, the queen gets to lead procession through the streets. The citizens also get to visit memorials to remember those who lost their lives during war.

The Trooping of the Colours

The trooping of the colours day takes place on the second Saturday every June. It is on this day that the citizens of England get to celebrate the birthday of their queen. The queen is honoured by being presented with a colourful parade from her soldiers. The soldiers always match on horseback. This festival is normally aired on television and millions of people in England and other parts of the world get to watch as well.

Bog Snorkeling

On this day participants wear goggles, flippers and snorkel and dive into a bog. They then race each other along a trench filled with nothing else but mud. The trench normally measures 120 ft. Participants come from different parts of the world and the money raised is taken to charity.

Ascot Ladies Day

Ascot is a small English town well known for horse racing. Ascot Racecourse is one of the leading race courses in UK. Today Ascot holds twenty five days of racing in one year. The biggest and most prestigious race takes place in June. The race is known as the King George VI and Queen Elizabeth stakes. What makes this race outstanding is that each unveiling year the hats get bigger, weirder and bolder.

Chapter 15: Local Markets

When it comes to fresh food, England has the best of many worlds. Having a long coastline and never-ending fresh fish as well as loads of farms, makes it easy to find fresh fruits and vegetables pretty much anywhere you go in the country. England has everything, from quaint little market towns out in the country to huge bustling farmers' markets in all of the bigger cities.

Gloucestershire

The Stroud Farmers' Market is one of the most famous in England. This market was primarily for butchers in the past but has evolved over the years to be an indoor and outdoor kind of market. It features a huge selection of local produce such as fresh fish, cheese, fruit and vegetables. One can also get clothing and jewellery but it is always crowded. The market is always open at from 8 AM on Wednesday, Friday and Saturday.

[For more information, visit fresh−n−local.co.uk]

Hampshire

Winchester Farmers Market, located in Hampshire, is one of the popular and biggest farmers' market in the United Kingdom which features over ninety vendors selling everything from meat to seafood. This market prides itself in the knowledge that all their products are locally produced as everything sold must come within 16 kilometers of Hampshire. There is a wide array of independent shops, boutiques and art galleries. This pedestrian friendly market is usually opened the second and last Sunday of every month from 9 AM to 2 PM.

[For more information, visit hampshirefarmersmarkets.co.uk]

Worcestershire

Teme Valley Market sells not only delicious local food but it is also has a pub so you can combine delicious food with a beer. This market has been running since 1998 making it one of the oldest famer's markets in the country and is situated in the heart of Worcestershire. This market is easily accessible with a free parking space. The market was established with the aim of bringing high quality country fare and goods to its locals.

[For more information, visit the—Talbot.co.uk]

Bristol, Bath, and Somerset

Located in Old town Bristol, the St. Nicholas Market focuses on food from around the world. The market is open six days a week and, on Wednesdays, there is a farmers' market where you can buy locally grown food. During the weekends, lovers of arts and crafts will get to add to their collection through the numerous displays sold on this days. It is open Monday through Saturday 9:30 AM to 5 PM. Bristol Farmers Market, on the other hand, opens on Wednesdays at 9:30 am to 2:30 pm and also offers the customers an opportunity to buy local fresh produce from the suppliers.

[For more information, visit stnicholasmarketbristol.co.uk]

North Yorkshire

Catterick Market goes beyond being a simple market. Along with selling amazing food, it also provides entertainment in the form of music, circus performances, and many other distractions. This market offers its locals as well as its visitors with a wide array of goods including rugs, cushions and even bikes. It is open every Sunday from 9 AM to 4 PM and it comes with a free entrance parking zone for its customers. People with disabilities also have their own car parking zone. Children are not left behind either, as there are numerous street entertainers and musicians doing various genres with live music provided at the Big Top. There's also an offer for Rock and Roll which will take you back to the good old days keeping you entertained while doing your shopping.

[For more information, visit cattericksundaymarket.co.uk]

Skipton Market will take you back in time as it is characterized by cobblestone streets which will make you feel like you're in a different century. The market also has a wide range of fresh farm produce. Your visit here will also provide you with an opportunity to access such sites as the Bolton Abbey, Skipton castle and boat rides along the Leeds through the Liverpool canal, which runs through the heart of the town. It is open Monday, Wednesday, Friday, and Saturday at 9 AM to 5 PM

[For more information, visit skiptonmarket.net]

London

Borough market is located on the banks of the River Thames in a spot that has not seen a market there since Roman times. It caters to adventurous foodies looking for exotic, expensive, and rare food items. The whole area surrounding the market is full of restaurants. The markets is the perfect spot for gourmet food and has more than 100 fish selling stalls, meat, cheese, cakes, vegetables and many more. The market hosts producers from all over the country who come and sell their fresh produce. It is usually open from Monday to Saturday with the full market operating from Wednesday to Saturday, while hot food traders, vegetable and fruit stalls can be found on Mondays and Tuesdays.

[For more information, visit boroughmarket.org.uk]

Portobello Road Market in London is well known and has been around since the 1800's. This market is accessible via the Ladbroke grove, Notting Hill Gate and the Westbourne Park tube station as well as the bus service routes servicing Notting Hill Gate and Ladbroke Grove.

The main market days are Fridays and Saturdays and the smaller ones running from Mondays to Thursdays.

You can also buy pretty much anything there from food to clothing to antiques and a variety of other offerings. It is open Monday through Thursday.

West Midlands

The Bull Ring, located in Birmingham, features the combination of haberdashery as well as an open air market, selling local fresh fruits and vegetables. Open Tuesday, Thursday, Friday, Saturday 9 AM to 5 PM. The market is characterized by 130 beautifully designed stalls around it creating a lively and attractive scene with the aim of attracting both customers and window shoppers. It's also particularly designed to accommodate those with disability.

[For more information, visit ragmarket.com]

Leicester

Leicester Market is huge and has the biggest outdoor covered market in all of Europe.

The outdoor market mostly deals with jewellery, fruits and vegetables, clothes and even second hand books, as well as permanent stalls dealing with cosmetics, greeting cards and many more. The indoor market established in 1973, on the other hand, deals with footwear, gemstones and even confectionary.

In the heart of the market is the Leicester corn exchange now serving as a bar/restaurant.

The market is usually open Monday to Saturday. A monthly farmers' market is now held on the last Wednesday of every month with a wide array of products including organic meat, fruits and vegetables.

[For more information, visit leicesxtermarket.co.uk]

Chapter 16: Festivals

English people love festivals and have been putting them on for centuries. Every year, new festivals are being created, celebrating everything from food to the arts to music to literature and film and beyond.

East Midlands

The Stamford Shakespeare Company, located in the adorable Lincolnshire town of Stamford, puts on a Shakespeare festival every summer, on the grounds of a mansion called Tolethorpe Hall.

Yorkshire

Yorkshire is a host to many festivals from January to January since time immemorial. In January, a two day York National Book Fair is carried out. Since 1974, this fair has become one of the biggest out-of-print book fair in United Kingdom.

Huddersfield Literature Festival is another successful event that was started in 2006. It welcomes several book enthusiast, authors and acts.

Another recent festival is the York Literature Festival, which was started in 2007. It takes place annually in March, opening its grounds to literary events such as cinema, poetry, workshops, performances, and theatre to one and all.

April ushers in the National Student Drama Festival. This is normally based in Scarborough. It started back in 1956 and was steered off by Kenneth Pearson, an arts columnist in the Sunday Times, Harold Hobson and Frank Copplestone. The event showcases the raw talent of 16-25 year olds.

FEVA is an annual festival that goes down in Knaresborough. It is a festival of entertainment and visual arts that offer a range of events, most of which are literary themed. The festival offers something for everyone in the family. There's free admission to the events.

Musicport is a large festival that takes place at the resort of Bridlington and features music from around the world. It takes place every November and draws large crowds.

Every August, the North Yorkshire town of Whitby hosts Whitby Folk Week. It attracts musicians from all over for a week of concerts and a variety of other performances and workshops.

Tramlines Festival is for festival goers looking for more of a party atmosphere, and it features hip-hop artists, dance music, house and electronic music, and other bands that make the crowd want to dance the night away. The festival is only a couple of years old and was originally free to the public. Tickets now cost money but are incredibly inexpensive. It takes place every July in Sheffield, South Yorkshire.

Oxfordshire

The Wilderness Festival at Cornbury Park in Oxfordshire is like a weekend camp where attendees can enjoy concerts, try food from around the world, see spoken word performances and talks, watch plays, go swimming, go fishing, take arts and crafts workshops, and an amazing variety of other options all over the course of a couple of days in August. The festival has only been going on for five years and is already proving to be incredibly popular especially with those festival goers that want a more mellow and natural environment, where they can camp for a few days.

Magna Carta Anniversary: Oxford's Bodleian Library annually holds a quarter of the Magna Carta manuscripts. These manuscripts date back to the 13th century.

Northeast

EAT! Newcastle is a huge food festival that takes place every August all over Newcastle and is a foodie's dream. There is also a winter version of the festival called EAT! IN, and features winter comfort food in cozy restaurants. It takes place at the end of February.

Another heart throbbing event in the North East is the Annual Oyster Festival, which was started in 2004. It is one of the most celebrated events in the social and corporate calendar of North East. Though it is a day at the races, no horses take part in the celebrations.

During this glamorous festival, ladies dress to kill while the gentlemen arrive to a champagne studded reception while dressed in smart suits. Upon arrival, the entertainment kicks off and normally the environment gets electric. The participants get to sample a 3-course fruits-de-mer menu, oyster stalls as well beer and wine.

Bristol, Bath, and Somerset

Perhaps the best-known festival in England is the Glastonbury Festival of Contemporary and Performing Arts. It is a huge music festival that takes place over a couple of days in June every year. It attracts world-renowned bands, as well as hundreds of thousands of people to a farm outside Glastonbury. It began in the 70's and was originally a small hippie concert but has grown in immense popularity and is now one of the largest annual festivals in the world. Tickets can be incredibly expensive and often sell out quickly.

Another festival, though not hugely celebrated, is the Slapstick Silent Comedy Festival. This annual event makes the city of Bristol appear brighter and sunnier in dark wintry January. It features silent comedies coupled with live musical entertainment as well as talks. It is usually held at the Colston Hall.

East Anglia

Latitude Festival, which started in 2006, is a music and arts festival that takes place over a long weekend every summer in Suffolk. It showcases a variety of music genres and a wide assortment of musicians, ranging from small local bands to huge international stars. It also has performances of other forms of entertainment, including stand-up comics, sketch comedy, dance groups, film premieres, slam poetry, theatrical performances, art installations, and talks by well-known authors, storytellers, and a whole host of other entertainers.

It attracts much smaller crowds then some of the more popular long-running festivals, and takes place over a few days every summer.

Norfolk and Norwich Festival is another old festival in the city dating back to 1824. It was initially held so as to raise funds for the Norfolk and Norwich Hospital. Back then, it was a classical musical event. Today, the festival includes a variety of dance, children's events and visual arts.

.

Chapter 17: British Cuisine & Restaurants

It is an old joke that the food in England is not very good. On the contrary, not only is some of traditional English food absolutely delicious, in England, one can find food from pretty much anywhere in the world. Many world-renowned restaurants and chefs can be found in England. Actually, there are so many amazing restaurants it was hard to narrow it down.

London is one of the food capitals of the world and is definitely the place to visit in England to find an amazing meal. In fact, pretty much all of the best restaurants in England are located in London.

It is overflowing with amazing restaurants and foodies from around the world visit there primarily to try as many of its famed restaurants as possible. The best part is that you can get an amazing meal without having to spend a fortune. Or if you want to spend a fortune on your meal, you can eat at some of the top ranked restaurants in the world. It will be the focus of the restaurant section because there is no other city in England that even comes close where food is concerned.

Indian cuisine is very popular among London culture and has become widely populated in the market.

Chinatown is in every major city in England, especially London, and offers an array of shops and restaurants that accommodate all of China's cuisine, you can buy pre-made food or ingredients (i.e. their popular desserts etc.) or you can go to nearby restaurants, a popular option is an all-you-can eat buffet.

England is well-known for its fish and chips. They use white cold fish, which they get from Scottish seas and are freshly prepared and battered in the shops. There are also some exclusive ''chippy's'' (fish and chip shops, as they like to call them) that hold the Michelin star honour for best fish and chips. The English love having their chips with a bit of salt and vinegar and dip it in ketchup and mayo.

Some Places to Visit

Gymkhana

- World famous for its delectable Indian cuisine. It is often voted as one of the best restaurants in the world. It also fuses the Indian delicacies with recipes of the modern day Great Britain.

- 42 Albemarle Street, London.

Dishoom

- Featuring amazing authentic Indian cuisine. It opened early in the last century by immigrants from Iran. Get a taste of the Irani cafes which were once a part of the life in Bombay. The staff is known to be very friendly. The prices here are low and the food is of top quality first class.

- 12 Upper St. Martin's plane, London

Gordon Ramsay

- Owned by the celebrity chef, has received many of the highest culinary awards for its modern French menu. It is, however, known for being incredibly expensive. It employs both modern and classic techniques and thus why it is outstanding. It initially started in 1998 in Chelsea. It can, at one time, host a total of 45 guests. Its stylish interiors were designed by Fabled Studio, crowning it with contemporary elegance. You do not have to be at the restaurant to view the menu. Get online and comfortably peruse through the menu and at the same time make an online booking.

- 68 Royal Hospital Road, London

Homeslice Pizza

- While being more affordable for the average traveler, it has gotten rave reviews for its wood fired pizza. Though it is incredibly popular and the wait might be long, it's worth it.

- 13 Neal's Yard, London

Regency Café

- It is an art deco style café that first opened in 1946. It has occasionally been used as a filming location. The original owners sold it to Antonio Perotti and Gino Schiavetta in 1986. It is currently owned by Antonio's daughter and Gino's son.

- It has an original tiling and the tables formica topped.

- Go here for a classic English breakfast.

- Despite being a casual café that is decently priced, it is consistently ranked one of the best places to eat in England.

- 17 Regency Street, London

Honest Burgers

- It was started in 2011 by Tom and Phil and wes inspired by British produce. They used to serve burgers at festivals and events before opening the restaurant.

- The two have not deviated from its original approach.

- Great place to get a plump and juicy burger at a decent price.

- 4A Meard St, London

Duck and Waffle

- Great restaurant to go to if you want an amazing view with your meal. It is located forty stories above London and serves classic British cuisine. It uses local, seasonal and sustainable ingredients from Britain.

- It operates on a 24 hour basis and offers late night menus.

- All its meals are prepared by its award winning Executive Chef Daniel Doherty.

- 110 Bishopsgate, London

Barrafina

- Likely the best place in London to get Spanish food, and you can get a great meal at a decent price.

- The restaurants have an open kitchen allowing the guest to see how their meals are prepared while on the red leather stools.

- Executive Head Chef Nieves Barragan Mohacho prepares a la carte menus.

- Bookings for groups can be made within a range of 8 to 32 persons on their private dining space.

- 54 Frith Street, London

Nightjar

- Old-school-cool lounge with a massive selection of cocktails and spirits as well as delicious appetizers and cheeses. It's got a jazz theme and offers live music. It is so popular that you can only get in by booking ahead of time.

- 129 City Road, London

Burger and Lobster

- Great place to get seafood or an upscale burger if you are in the mood for American food. There is also a New York location of this restaurant.

- 36 Dean St., London

Flat Iron

- Good place to get a great steak at a decent price. It is consistently ranked as one of the best steakhouses in the United Kingdom.

- 17 Beak St. London

Chapter 18: Accommodations

Whether you are traveling in luxury or on a shoestring budget, it's always important to find a comfortable and safe place to stay when you're traveling.

London

The Morgan House, located in Victoria is a lovely B&B at a decent price, and comes with a full breakfast. The hotel is centrally placed and minutes away from the Victoria train and tube station. The guesthouse is also surrounded by scenic sites such as the Buckingham palace and is one of the safest hotels to book yourself in.

[For more information, visit Morgan House.co.uk]

Hoxton Hotel, in the East End offers inexpensive modern accommodations that include breakfast. This hotel has literally done away with things that annoy its customers such as expensive mini-bars, high rate phone calls and unpaid internet. They also have partnership with the Soho House where its guests can interact with the locals.

[For more information, visit hoxtonhotels.com]

Clink 78 is a huge hostel in a Victorian building aimed towards young travellers. They have a bar and breakfast included with an extremely cheap room rate. This hostel can accommodate over 500 guests and has an onsite basement bar where guests can go and unwind. It also offers its guests a chance to meet and mingle with other travellers.

[For more information, visit clinkhostels.com]

Southeast

For those seeking old-fashioned charm, there is the Rookery Nook in Shere near Guildford, which is in a tiny cottage from the 15th-century. Rates are extremely reasonable with the en-suite package accompanied by a free parking space, internet and complimentary tea and coffee facilities. The breakfast room allows the guests an ample time to prepare their snacks or eat their takeaways. For evening strolls for fresh air, guests are welcome to use the conservatory gardens.

[For more information, visit rookerynook.info]

Drakes Hotel at the beach in Brighton is for those who can afford a little luxury and are willing to splurge on a great location. The rooms here are attractively designed and furnished with the beddings handcrafted with lush fabrics for maximum comfort. The hotel will provide you with an unforgettable fine dining experience as evidenced by the chef's talents accompanied by exquisite cocktails with an amazing view of the sea.

[For more information, visit drakesofbrighton.com]

Devon & Cornwall

In the port town of Boscastle is a great youth hostel located on a lovely river. This hostel is clean and comfortable, with great rates. This area is, however, prone to floods as witnessed in 2004 and 2007.

This village has a 20-mile harbor protected by 2 stone harbor walls. While here, one can visit the Museum of Witchcraft and the Boscastle pottery.

[For more information, visit yha.org.uk]

East Midlands

Located in the lovely town of Stamford is the George Hotel, which is a beautiful building full of antiques, making it one of the best coaching inns in England though it is a bit expensive.

The hotel is accompanied by a distinctive style ad a serene environment making it a unique guest house. It is characterized by roaring log fires, afternoon teas, and a garden room as well as an oak paneled restaurant. The rooms, on the other hand, are tastefully decorated to provide you with refined luxury.

[For more information, visit georgehotelofstamford.com]

Cumbria

The Carlile City Hostel located in Carlisle is neat and clean in a great location at a very good price. This hostel is great as it caters for backpackers, walkers, cyclists and even tourists. It even offers a communal kitchen for its guests to prepare the breakfast as well as dinner, or to prepare packed lunch for those going sightseeing in the area. Guests will also enjoy free Wi-Fi in the communal areas and bicycle and bag storage areas.

[For more information, visit carlislecityhostel.com]

Yorkshire

Gallery B&B, near North York Moors, is a gorgeous 18th-century building on Main Street for a very good price. The formerly well known art gallery now offers you spacious self-contained boutique cottage for two fitted with stylish furniture with a touch of modern design. It also harbors a spa for unwinding with quality organic products and has a perfect view of the gardens and the farmland.

The hotel also offers an opportunity for walks through the rainforest walk, Cloudehill gardens and the rhododendron gardens close by.

[For more information, visit gallerybedandbreakfast.co.uk]

Northumberland Coast

No 1. Sallyport is an absolutely luxurious B&B located in Berwick and is in a house from the 17th century. Booking comes with dinner every night.

[For more information, visit sallyport.co.uk]

Northwest

The Radisson Blu Edwardian located in Manchester is a five star modern hotel with plenty of luxury to go around if you have the money to spend. These are a collection of luxury hotels in prime locations in the heart of London and Heathrow. They have very luxurious individually designed bedrooms and conference rooms with contemporary restaurants designed to meet the needs of every guest to make their stay worthwhile.

[For more information, visit radissonblu-edwardian.com]

Hilton Chambers Hostel is a new building located in downtown Manchester and it has absolutely comfortable accommodations at an incredibly low price. This hotel is at the heart of the northern quarter of Manchester city's centre. This guest house offers free breakfast as well as free Wi-Fi in the communal areas for its guests. It caters for all groups of people and can accommodate private dining, conferences and meetings.

Weekday events include game nights, film nights as well as a free tour of Manchester city by the hostel's knowledgeable staff.

The hostel also offers both shared and private en-suite rooms and is within a walking distance to Manchester Piccadilly station and Metrolink services.

[For more information, visit hattersgroup.com/Hilton]

Northeast

The Jesmond Dene House in Jesmond is luxury in a forest surrounding. It's a very popular hotel in the area all thanks to the stylish interiors and luxury accommodations in a parkland centre. The hotel is conveniently located in that it is a 5-minute drive from the city centre.

The rooms are individually designed in that neither the rooms nor the views look the same and are all furnished with a modern touch.

[For more information, visit jesmonddenehouse.co.uk]

Sleeperz in Newcastle is located in the middle of town and offers great rooms for the right price. This guesthouse will guarantee you a comfortable stay accompanied by the friendly atmosphere all thanks to the ever friendly staff.

The rooms are all air conditioned and there is access to uninterrupted access to the internet due to the free Wi-Fi for the guests. You will also find the rooms are heated, coupled with a power shower and anti-steam mirrors.

[For more information, visit sleeperz.com/Newcastle]

West Midlands

Old House Suites in Shropshire is a wonderful historical house which can cater for your accommodation at a decent rate.

The hotel offers spacious guestrooms accompanied by petite or full gourmet kitchens, fireplaces, and soaker tubs among others, that will guarantee you a comfortable stay.

It's located along the Courtney River and is close to dinning, shopping and championship golf courses and other recreational facilities. You can also enjoy such activities as mountain biking, kayaking or skiing during your stay

[For more information, visit theoldhousesuites.com]

Chapter 19: A Few Last Words

It's easy to see that England offers a huge variety of attractions for travellers. For a relatively small country, it has an incredible array of cultures, traditions, festivals, and outdoor activities. Each region is unique in its own way, has its own dialect, and its own way of life.

You could spend months traveling the country and still only see a small portion of what it has to offer.

No matter what kind of activities you are seeking, they can probably be found in England. Whether you are interested in a relaxing vacation at the beach or if you want to go on a long hiking and camping trip through an ancient forest, or if you are looking for a thriving nightlife and club scene, they can all be found in England.

No matter what your dream vacation is, you can find it in England. With the help of this guide, you may just be able to make it the vacation of a lifetime.

PS: Can I Ask You For A Special Favor?

Hopefully this guidebook has given you some ideas about what to do during your stay in England!!

We would like to ask you for a favor, would you be kind enough to leave a review for this book on Amazon? It'd be greatly appreciated!

Thanks a lot.

Preview of "Barcelona - By Locals"

We edit and publish travel guides from several cities in the world, all written by locals. When you plan your next destiny, please check on Amazon if we are covering that city already. If not, we will probably writing about it soon, please give us some time.

We would like to give you an advance of our Barcelona Guide, which is very special. Please take a look:

Chapter 1: Preface

Spain is defiantly among the world's favorite destinations. The rich history, gorgeous kilometer long beaches, magnificent architecture and warm climate attract millions of tourist every year.

Its crown jewel is indubitably Barcelona. Located on the northeastern Mediterranean coast of Spain, Barcelona attracts almost 10 million tourists every year alone. The Catalan capital has become a theme park for tourists, offering a huge variety of things worth seeing and doing and covering every tourist's taste.

Although the number of tourists in Barcelona can leave you feeling somewhat overwhelmed, the city should definitely be on your must-visit list. La Rambla, a wide tree-lined boulevard is crowded with tourists at almost any time of the year. Souvenirs shops, restaurants and money changers sit side by side. The number of bars and restaurants in the city centre has tripled from 200 to 600 in the last seven years, over flooding the streets with tables and chairs.

Founded as a Roman city, nowadays Barcelona is one of the world's leading tourists, economic, trade fair and cultural centers. Its influence in commerce, education, entertainment, media, fashion, science, and the arts contribute to its status as one of the world's major global cities. In 2009 the city was ranked Europe's third and one of the world's most successful as a city brand. In the same year the city was ranked Europe's fourth best city for business and fastest improving European city.

Barcelona is the 10th-most-visited city in the world and the third most visited in Europe after London and Paris. With its Rambles, Barcelona is ranked the most popular city to visit in Spain. It's an internationally renowned a tourist destination, with numerous recreational areas, one of the best beaches in the world, mild and warm climate, historical monuments, including eight UNESCO World Heritage Sites, many good-quality hotels, and developed tourist infrastructure.

Chapter 2: Benvinguda!

Barcelona is very well connected to the rest of Europe. There are plenty of flights, ships or trains leading to Barcelona. Getting there by bus or car is also a good idea as there are several main roads leading to Barcelona from France and Spain. The traffic outside of rush hours is usually light and it's possible to find free parking spaces a few metro stops from the city center.

If you chose to fly to Barcelona, consider choosing one of the nearby airports, instead of Barcelona - El Prat

International Airport. Airports in Girona, nearly 100 km to the north, or Reus, around the same distance to the south are a great alternative to Barcelona International Airport as you can find flights for €35 from Paris, London or Brussels. Both of them are conveniently connected to Barcelona and the trip to the city center would take around an hour.

For Girona Airport, the Barcelona Bus service runs a shuttle bus from Estació del Nord (which is in walking distance to the Arc de Triomf metro stop) in Barcelona to Girona. A one-way ticket costs €16 and a return ticket costs €25. The journey takes approximately one hour and ten minutes. Timetables are available on-line.

For Reus Airport, the easiest way to get there is to take the bus run by Hispano Igualadina. It will take you to Barcelona Sants bus station. Bus departures are synchronized with Ryanair plane departures/arrivals. One way ticket costs €13 and a return ticket costs €24. The journey takes c. 100 min, depending on the traffic on the motorway. Timetables are available on-line.

Barcelona—El Prat Airport is located 12 km southwest of the centre of Barcelona. This is the second largest airport in Spain, behind Madrid Barajas Airport. This is also one of the busiest airports in the world. There are now two terminals, T1 and T2 which are linked by a bus shuttle service, going every 5-7 minutes.

T1 was opened in 2009 and it's the fifth largest in the world. Terminal 2 is divided into three linked sections, known as Terminal 2A, 2B and 2C. Terminal 2B is the oldest part of the complex still in use, dating back to 1968. Terminals 2A and 2C were added in order to expand the airport capacity before the arrival of the Olympic Games in Barcelona in 1992.

Getting from the airport to the city center is pretty easy. There is a shuttle bus service that connects the Airport (both terminals) with the centre of Barcelona. Aerobús leaves every 5-10 minutes from T1 (A1) and every 10-20minutes from T2 (A2). The shuttle bus service is available every day from 5:30am to 1am, and the journey lasts about 30 minutes (although it can take considerably longer during rush hour). From the Airport, the shuttle bus makes a total of 4 stops: Plaça

Espanya, Gran Via - Urgell, Plaça Universitat, and finally Plaça de Catalunya. A one-way ticket to/from either Terminal costs €5.90 or you can buy a return ticket for €10.20 which is valid for 9 days.

If you happen to arrive between 1am and 5:30am, you can use Nitbús night bus service instead of Aerobús. Line N17 to T1 or line N16 to T2 departs every 20 min from 10pm to 6am. The ride from the Airport to Plaça de Catalunya takes about 40-50 min.

The cheapest, but slower option than Aerobús, is a bus 46 serving both T1 & T2. Its last stop in Barcelona is Plaça Espanya reached in 25-30 minutes. The one-way ticket costs €2 and can be purchased from the driver. If you have to transfer using the metro, tram or another bus, get a T10 Travelcard from the vending machine located at the train station outside Terminal 2. This card is valid for 75 minutes.

Between 11pm and 6am the 46 bus service is replaced by N16/17 buses; they take a diversion adding some ten minutes to the travel time, ending at Plaça Espanya.

A cheap and fast option to get to the city from the airport is the half-hourly RENFE R2 Nord suburban train line arriving at Sants (travel time: 18 min), Passeig de Gràcia (24 min), El Clot-Aragó (30 min) and more stations beyond Barcelona city limits. The train terminals are located next to T2 by section B, with a connecting green colored bus service to T1. If you arrive at T1, you'll need to catch the free airport transfer bus which stops right next to the Aerobús stop. The ride takes around 10 minutes.

A single journey ticket costs €4.10, but you can also buy a T10 Travelcard for €10.30. The card is valid for ten trips over any period of time; each of those trips includes 3 bus, metro, train or tramway transfers made within 75 min. You can buy a T10 from the ticket vending machine at the airport station and at the tobacco shop in front of Terminal 2B or at T1 in the tobacco shop just outside the arrival lounge exit.

If you are not a fan of public transportation, you can use a taxi to take you wherever you need to go. You can pre book a taxi online. A taxi ride to the city center costs around €30-40.

Instead of flying, you could also reach Barcelona by train. Several trains per day including overnight hotel trains from other parts of Europe (via France) are regular and reliable. As up 2013 there is also a high-speed line between Barcelona and Figueres. The new SNCF and RENFE cooperation offers service between cities in France and Barcelona.

Another option is a ferry or cruise ship. You can use a boat to Barcelona from the Balearic Islands, Genoa, Rome, Livorno, Sardinia, Tangier, and Algiers. The boat ride from Rome to Barcelona is actually cheaper than the bus. The city's port is one of the busiest on the Mediterranean, with nine passenger terminals, seven for cruise liners and four for ferries.

A car or a bus is also a good option. There are several main roads leading to Barcelona from France and Spain and traffic is usually relatively light outside of peak hours. If you happen to travel with your car keep in mind that blue parking spots are being charged from Monday to Saturday, 9am to 2pm and 4pm to 6pm. Anyone can use a blue space but they aren't that easy to find. You pay at the meter and put the ticket on the dashboard. Green parking spaces are for residents only while white parking spaces are free of charge at all times but there aren't any in the city centre.

Made in the USA
Lexington, KY
25 April 2019